More into Africa

With

3 kids, some dogs and a husband

ANN PATRAS

The ongoing adventures of a young family who went to live and work in Zambia for two years – and stayed a while longer.

Book 2 of the 'Africa' series.
Also available as an ebook.

Table of Contents

Note

Into Africa should not be considered as a regular travel guide, nor does it provide an in-depth look at African culture. It describes my life in Zambia, based on letters written in 1980/81.

I am not and never have been a racist. There are good and bad people of all colours, creeds and nationalities, and I am pleased to say that attitudes have changed dramatically in Africa since the era of this book.

I have what I like to think of as a 'typically British' dry sense of humour, which occasionally people may not recognise as humour, and does include the occasional mild swear word.

It should be noted that, in the interest of authenticity, conversations and observations contained in this book reflect what was said, assumed or apparent to me *at that time*.

Dedicated

To ZIGGY,

without whom none of this would have happened.

X

1

Homeward Bound

"Mummy, I'm going to be sick."

Here we go again, I thought.

"Brad, is this the 'I'm going to be sick' like when we were on the plane flying into Africa? But then you weren't sick," I asked. "Or is it like the 'I'm going to be sick' when you actually were sick, all down the back of the taxi driver's seat four weeks ago?"

"I don't know, Mummy."

To be on the safe side I reached for the paper bag from the pouch in the aircraft seat in front of me, and handed it to my eldest son.

"Be a good boy and if you think you're going to be sick, be sick into this," I said to him. "Then take it to the nice lady wearing the hat."

I hoped he realised I meant the air stewardess, not the passenger three seats down wearing colourful headgear which matched her African sarong. I must sound like a dreadful mother, instructing my not yet five-year-old son to dispose of his own sick bag, but one of the things about motherhood I just could not come to grips with was child vomit. It had a detrimental effect on my own health.

Otherwise my motherly skills weren't so bad, considering I gave birth to twins when Brad was only 17 months old. Three children within eighteen months is quite a challenge. Taking them, and all your possessions, as you accompany your husband to work and live in Africa, is another. In 1980 my husband Ziggy accepted a two year contract to work in Zambia. When we left England behind we had no idea what to expect, and if we had, I doubt we would have gone. But once we acknowledged and accepted the vagaries of this strange, hot country and slowed down our inner tempo to fit the dawdling African pace, we found we thoroughly enjoyed it.

During our first year in Kitwe, Brad had developed ear problems. Luckily we managed to get Rhinestone, Ziggy's employers, to pay for a midterm return trip to the UK for surgery which was unavailable in Zambia. A lot of things were not available in Zambia, but I won't go into that now.

Our sudden unannounced appearance at the Burton Arms, my parents' pub, on the 1st August had caused great excitement all round, though our three-and-a-bit weeks stay seemed very short. It was even shorter for Ziggy, who had to return a week earlier than the kids and I, due to pressures of work. No big deal, you would think. But not so enthralling for me when I had to make the long, three-legged journey back to Kitwe on my own, with our three small children in tow, plus belongings.

On the main Heathrow to Lusaka twelve-hour flight we had been allocated seats near the front of the economy section. Brad soon discarded his unused sick bag and settled down to fight nicely with his brother and sister. The long, narrow, stainless steel trolley, attended by two Zambian hostesses (as they were called then), had begun its front to back service down the single central aisle, dispensing the customary chicken and beef. I had just returned to my seat after cutting up the kids' food, when Brad hit me with his next blow.

"Mummy, I need a wee."

"Well, can't it wait until you've eaten your dinner?" I asked him.

"No, Mummy."

"Yes, it can. Get on with your dinner."

I think he managed two spoonfuls of rice before, "Mummy, I really, *really* need a wee."

I asked the man next to me if he would be so kind as to hold my tray while I extricated myself from my seat. Once out I repositioned the little fold-down table for my food, onto which he placed my tray, none too gently, before returning his attention to his own dinner.

I unfastened Brad from his seat and walked to the nearest hostess, who was serving food to people three rows back.

"I'm terribly sorry," I said, "but my little boy urgently needs to go to the toilet. Would you mind bringing your trolley up this way, just for a moment, so that he can get past?"

"No, he will have to wait," she replied.

"But it really *is* urgent."

"Try First Class," she said, then turned away. "Chicken or beef?"

"Charming," I muttered, and turned back to Brad.

Time for plan B.

"Okay, Sunshine, let's try up here," I said to my son.

Taking him by the hand, I approached the beige curtain which separated us from First Class and peeked through.

I could see the toilet just on the other side of the aircraft's First Class galley, and crept towards it, ushering Brad in front of me. I'd got him inside and was about to close the door when a harsh voice demanded my attention.

"What do you think you are doing here?"

The hostess ran up and pushed me away from the door, then she noticed Brad. She grabbed his hand and pulled him out of the cubicle.

"You cannot use this toilet. You are not First Class passengers!" she hissed, as she shoved us back to the curtain.

"You cannot come through this curtain. It is private to First Class passengers only, and you are not a first class person!"

I tried to explain to her that he was just a little boy who urgently needed the toilet, and that we couldn't reach the toilets in economy for ages due to the trolley service.

"That is not my problem."

And with a swish and flurry of cloth, the curtain closed. We were dismissed.

Now I was getting cross.

"Mummeeeeee," wailed Brad "I have to *go!*"

Time for Plan C.

I returned to the trolley dollies who were now three rows further down the aircraft, but still nowhere near half way along.

"Excuse me, we weren't allowed to use the First Class toilets. Could you please pass my son over to your colleague and he will take himself to the toilet at the back?"

I picked Brad up to pass him to her.

"I am busy," she said. "Chicken or beef?"

So I held Brad up to shoulder level.

"Could any passenger back there," I called out, "please take this child off me so that he can go to the toilet?"

After a short delay, which seemed to go on forever whilst I held a 4-year-old child in the air, a man stood up to take him.

I stretched as far as I could, somewhat hindered by the hostess and her loaded trolley. At the moment of handover, the trolley dolly on the bloke's side turned from her chicken and beefing to find a child in her face, and in the moment of surprise, knocked Brad's bum with her shoulder. All efforts by myself and the knight in shining armour to hold Brad aloft went in vain, and Brad tumbled from our grips.

But he didn't fall far, just onto the head of a lady in a seat between us, who had just removed the lid from her chicken curry. Brad squeaked and the woman screamed as she stared down at the chicken curry now spreading down the front of her dress.

"I'm terribly sorry," I said to the poor woman, "I really am. But blame the hostesses for this. They refused to help in any way. I'm truly sorry this happened to you."

She glared at the mess and then at me.

"You should have made the child wait!" she shouted.

I returned to my seat, now not feeling in the least bit guilty about her discomfort. With an attitude like that I figured she deserved what she got.

It was about 20 minutes before Brad returned from the toilet, having been made to wait until all the meals had been served to the rest of the passengers. He then rushed back to me.

"Everybody was really nice back there, Mummy. People kept asking me if I was alright, and wanted to know what happened, so I told 'em. They thought it was ever so funny!"

The remainder of the flight was uneventful, but strangely lacking in cabin service. So when I wanted a drink I simply walked down to the rear galley, opened the cupboards till I found what I wanted, and took it back to my seat. None of the crew said a word.

I was never so happy as when I saw Ziggy's smiling face at the bottom of the steps when we tumbled out of the small Zambia Airways plane which had carried us on our final leg from Lusaka to Kitwe. With some considerable difficulty he managed to cram us all, plus our four suitcases and hand baggage, into the company car, and as we caught up on some of our news, the kids talked about everything they were going to do once they got 'home'.

* * * * *

Home was a bungalow in the residential suburb of Riverside in Kitwe, the main mining town of Zambia's Copperbelt Region.

Our house was set in a large garden containing several fruit trees. It had four bedrooms, two bathrooms, a nice lounge with connecting dining room, and a big kitchen with an attached scullery. It was referred to, by us, as the Big House in contrast to a temporary, smaller, 'borrowed' house we stayed at on our initial arrival in Kitwe, which we called the Little House.

Our home was maintained, five and a half days a week, by our trusty house-servant, Benton, who lived in the small house, known as a *khaya*, in a corner of our garden, with his wife and two and a half children (Christina was expecting).

I must confess that when we first heard that, a 'house servant' would be provided, I was adamant that I would not succumb to such colonial practices. It only took me a few weeks, after our arrival in the country, to discover that home help was not a colonial luxury, but a practical necessity.

There were no carpets. Floors had to be swept and mopped daily. There were no washing machines. Most of the washing was done in the bath and every single item of clothing, as well as bed sheets and towels, had to be ironed before use. This was to avoid maggots growing under your skin from the putzi fly which laid its eggs in damp washing that then infiltrated one's skin.

Anyway, where was I? Oh, yes…

I said Benton was 'trusty' to differentiate him from some of the servants we had employed during the previous year, in both household and other capacities, who had turned out to be considerably less reliable for various reasons, and whose employment it had been necessary to curtail.

In-depth accounts of their diverse inadequacies or transgressions were extensively described in my first book, *Into Africa: with 3 Kids, 13 Crates and a Husband.*

Ziggy's employers also paid for a guard to be present on the property each night from 6pm to 6am. This security was additional to having all opening windows protected by burglar bars, an almost six foot high wall all around the garden and solid gates which were kept locked at all times.

When I'd first heard about the guard facility, I had thought it was protection against marauding lions or rampaging elephants, but it appeared to be a precaution against thieves, of which there appeared to be no shortage in the Zambian cities. A sad state of affairs, but true.

Completing the household were our three dogs, a highly pedigreed Irish setter officially titled Rosscarbery's Ruby Prince, who we called Coke, and two black-and-tan medium-sized dogs of dubious parentage named Sally and Foxwell. These two we had adopted from friends who had left Rhinestone rather suddenly the month before we went on our UK trip.

Ziggy had been contracted for two years as Site Manager on the building of the new Cobalt Processing Plant, commissioned by Zambia Consolidated Copper Mines, affectionately known as ZCCM.

Rhinestone had offered a pretty good deal. They provided the house (and paid all the utility bills and servants' wages), a company car, private medical facilities, and schooling for the kids. They also paid for our membership of two social clubs, a serious necessity due to the lack of pubs.

When we had first arrived in Zambia we were horrified to discover that pubs did not exist for our enjoyment. Where were we going to socialise, and drink? Then we discovered there was a plethora of sports and social clubs, one of which became our 'second home', the Nkana Kitwe Arts Society, or NKAS, or the Little Theatre, or Theatre Club, and commonly referred to (by us) as *The Club*. Not that we had any thespian talents but,

- it was the first club we visited,
- it had a lovely pool and play area for the kids,
- it had a nice bar and friendly members.

What more could we ask for? It also came with some catches. Members were expected to 'pull their weight' by helping out in whatever field they could, on stage, backstage, front of house, in fact all sorts of areas. Being the idiot that I am, I mentioned I could sew. I virtually lived in the Club's 'Wardrobe' after that. (No, it wasn't a large wooden cabinet, but a big room, backstage, with rails packed with dresses and jackets, and shelves crammed full of cardboard boxes full of other clothes, hats and shoes.)

Ziggy found that quite a few of his colleagues at work enjoyed membership of the Cricket Club, so we joined that too. Fortunately there were no obligations for that other than to have a mild interest in cricket and a generous interest in drinking, so we easily qualified there.

As I said earlier, we had absolutely no idea what to expect when we moved to Zambia. We soon found that Kitwe was home to a well-established expatriate community. To be honest I was so naïve in the ways of the world, as opposed to the ways of my hometown of Burton upon Trent, that before arriving in Zambia I had never even heard the expression 'ex-pat'. You would think that, having spent a year living in Canada before I got married, I would have come across it. On the contrary, there I was classified as an immigrant.

Such was the camaraderie in Kitwe that many of the ex-pats became almost part of the family, as I learned how to cope and enjoy the new and very different lifestyle I needed to adapt to.

Having spent most of my life in a brewery town in England, I quickly came to love the wide open spaces which came with living in Africa. The hot, sunny weather was the stuff dreams were made of, and I was delighted to be living mine.

2
Back to Normal

The reason we were in Zambia in the first place was simple. Work.

Before we came to live in Zambia my husband's job in the petrochemical industry had seen him working quite a long way from home, to the extent that he would leave for work on a Monday morning, only returning on a Friday, late afternoon. When the division of the company he worked for was closed down, a small redundancy payment allowed time for him to search for a job where he could return home every night.

The trouble was, positions open to him in the petro-chem field were nearly all coastal based. Our home base of Burton upon Trent was in the very centre of England, which would mean us moving house to be together. This was not a practical option as the project specialities he worked on rarely lasted longer than several months. So, in the middle of 1980, he applied for and got the job in Zambia, which offered a two year contract, with the possibility of extension.

Our first year in Zambia had found us rather astonished by the lack of basic essential commodities. I could frequently be seen standing alongside scores of patient Zambian women, waiting in queues to buy simple things such as soap, washing powder, flour, cooking oil, salt and sugar. There was no such thing as convenience food. The nearest we got to that was cans of baked beans and tinned corned beef which, incidentally, was the best I had ever tasted. I think those two items came from Zimbabwe next door.

Zambia in the early 1980s was not self-sufficient. There were no processed food stuffs being produced in the country, unless you count beer. Most things beyond milk, meat, vegetables and maize (the African staple diet) were imported from South Africa and had not easily been reaching Zambia because of the recent Bush War of Rhodesia, which lay between the two countries. Rhodesia became Zimbabwe, which only emerged as an independent country in April of 1980. Whilst the transportation of supplies was no longer such a problem, there was a marked lack of foreign exchange in Zambia with which to buy them.

Zambia's only significant export was copper, which hardly generated sufficient foreign exchange to fund the country's requirements of basic commodities. As a result, whenever Zambia's expats had people visiting from overseas, they were generally charged with bringing as many luxury items as they could cram into their cases.

Perhaps I should define luxury items. These were things such as Bisto, Oxo cubes, Marmite, cheese, HP sauce, tomato ketchup, spices, dried fruit, baking powder, cake decorations and candles, colouring for icing, cocoa powder, paper cake cases, tin foil, cling wrap, freezer bags, music tapes, make-up, nail polish and nail polish remover, good quality film for cameras, and batteries not past their sell-by dates. The list went on and on.

During our first year in Kitwe, all three of our kids had attended the Round Table pre-primary school. When Brad turned five in the October, he was eligible to attend the 'big school', Lechwe Primary, from the beginning of the new school year in September 1981.

One of the privileges of attending Lechwe included the wearing of their distinctive school uniform. The theme was chocolate brown for shorts and skirts, beige or yellow for shirts, blouses and dresses. Very nice, you would think. So did I, initially.

Almost every State school in Zambia had grey as its base colour, usually with pale blue or white shirts. Trying to find anything brown and beige was akin to looking for a pink elephant. In fact I think I've seen more pink elephants in my time.

I was quite handy with a sewing machine, but when you couldn't locally find the right fabric to put under the needle it was a superfluous skill. Fortunately I had heard about this uniform dilemma prior to our trip to the UK so had stocked up with metres of suitable fabric from my favourite stalls at Burton's Thursday market.

Within days of arriving home I was kept busy making uniforms. As I anticipated, as soon as Vicki and Leon saw Brad's in progress they had pleaded with me to have uniforms too, so I was sewing for all three of them.

This milestone event, of course, wouldn't be complete without a photograph.

Before we went away on leave I had been approached by Paul McDermott, one of the theatre members and a great producer, and asked if I would do the costumes for his next play. I had 'done the costumes' for a previous play of his and whilst he was a tough taskmaster, at the end of the day one got a great sense of achievement when working with him, so I said yes, then thought no more about it.

Not twenty-four hours had elapsed, after we returned to Zambia from our UK trip, before Paul phoned me to affirm my promise. A couple of days later we met at the Club and he showed me pictures of what he wanted. I wish I'd seen them before I'd agreed to do it. Bloody Norah!

The play turned out to be Schiller's *Mary Stuart*. Accommodating a cast of twenty-plus actors, the costumes were heavy Elizabethan, regaled with ruffs, leg o' mutton sleeves, tight 'v' waisted bodices, and full skirts or ornate doublet and hose. Oh, lordy.

It made the time I had spent on the previous play (and won an award for) look like an afternoon of hemming hankies.

To give him his due, Paul did arrange for us to go along to two other theatre clubs at the nearby towns of Chingola and Ndola to see if they had costumes we could borrow, but sadly they had little in that line.

I gathered around me a team of willing ladies who worked their fingers to the bone helping put everything together. Before this I had never actually seen a 'ruff' up close, now I had to figure out how to make dozens of them as collars and cuffs for the collection of costumes needed. These turned out to be the easy bits which could be done sitting beside the pool or while watching TV.

Not surprisingly, Queen Elizabeth caused the most work, with her various costume changes throughout the play, all of which were very lavish and presented quite a few logistical problems, until I realised that most of her dresses could be made out of curtain or upholstery fabric and braids.

The first dress rehearsal saw almost as many helpers as cast behind the scenes trying to shove, pin or tie people into their costumes. For the final week before the show went live I was putting in sixteen hour stints at the theatre, carting my sewing machine and all relevant accoutrements there and back each day. By the last dress rehearsal, two days before opening, we were sorted. Or at least the cast were.

Unfortunately I did it again, and landed myself with a rather strange commitment which meant I had to do sudden alterations to a dress on my one day off. Let me try to explain the scenario, which involved a pair of curtains on the set.

The curtains were hung from a large rectangular shaped rail. One side of the curtains looked just like curtains, but the other side was covered with a tapestry. During certain acts the curtains sat along the front rail, but during another set they hung from the back rail, so when stretched out along the wall, looked like a tapestry.

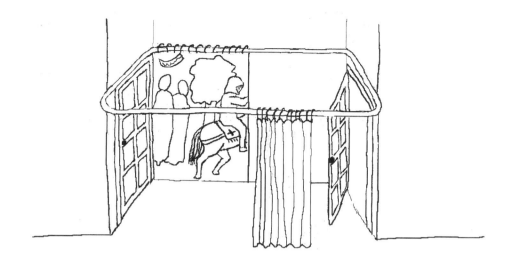

So what? you might ask. Well, the problem lay with the fact that between acts, the scenery, props and curtains had to be changed, and these changes took place before the eyes of the audience, insofar as we didn't close the main stage curtains.

Because of this, all the to-ing and fro-ing of stuff had to be done in semi-darkness by people in costume, which for the most part meant members of the cast (plus one props girl in costume).

It was the job of two page boys to pull the double sided curtains into position but, on the eve of the opening, Crispin, the stage manager, said they were having a helluva job getting them to go round the rectangular rail, and said he thought they'd have to cancel the idea of moving them at all, thus abandoning the tapestry part.

When I heard this I was absolutely horrified. The woman who had put the tapestry together had poured hours into it and had done a magnificent job. I expressed my opinion (rather vocally) saying I was sure there must be a solution.

In a few minutes I was on the stage with a broom handle and proceeded to carefully push the curtain rings round the rail.

"There you go, Crispin. Problem solved," I said with a smug grin.

"But there's another problem," he sighed.

"What now?"

"The page boys wouldn't possibly have time to fiddle with them like that, as they have other jobs to do as well."

"Then get someone else to do it."

"We don't have anyone else available," he replied.

"Okay then, *I'll* do it!"

Big mistake, because he held me to it. And I found myself frantically altering a suitable dress for me to wear before I made my stage debut as a stage hand. Never again!

One thing Crispin had failed to mention to me initially was that there was only a ninety second slot allowed for the set change. On the Opening night, as I stood in the wings at the end of the first act, I was wetting myself.

As the lights dimmed to half strength I took a deep breath and walked quickly on stage gripping my trusty pole. I poked it into the end curtain rings on the left side and began to push them along the rail when all of a sudden *bam!* I almost got hit in the face by an opening door.

Nobody had thought to mention to me that people would be using the door to access the stage during the scene changes. I abandoned that curtain temporarily and went over to shift the one on the right side. The rings started to get all jammed up as I was pushing it round the corner when *whoosh* the other blasted door opened and I nearly got knocked off my feet by a page boy carrying a chair!

I went back to the other side, which was now clear of egressing bodies and managed to get the curtain where it needed to go, then returned to the stuck one. I finally managed to get it round the bend by whacking the rings with the pole. As I shuffled the curtain into place the rapidly fading between-scenes music was competing with frantic whispers.

"Get off! Get off!" was heard coming from the actors standing behind those dratted doors, waiting to make their entrance.

By the time I'd finished my legs were shaking so much I could hardly stand and my heart was beating so furiously I thought I might have a heart attack. Only then did I find out that I had to carry out this procedure three times during the course of the play, once in reverse.

By the time the final curtain came down I was a nervous wreck.

To make matters worse I still had my 'regular job' (that of wardrobe mistress) to perform. Never a night went by without at least one costume mess-up occurring. Only the scale of severity varied.

* * * * *

It was the aim of the theatre to put on twelve productions a year, excluding the Sunday cinema. Most plays ran for two weekends, from Wednesday or Thursday to Saturday, so it was quite a busy place.

A lot of people were involved with the various productions but there was a core of about twenty or so stalwarts who somehow got roped into nearly everything that was going on. Ziggy and I seemed to fall into that category. Looking back, I wonder how some people had time to actually go to work.

NKAS had the incredible capacity to lure one in. We somehow managed to commit ourselves to more than wardrobe and backstage work.

Ziggy occasionally helped out front-of-house, welcoming patrons, checking tickets, directing to seats, and I found myself volunteering to help with catering at certain functions.

I don't know how we got landed with this one, but we also organised the weekly Sunday Film, me selling the tickets and Ziggy selecting and hiring the films, sourcing and displaying posters, and being the projectionist.

I regularly checked Ziggy and looked at myself in the mirror to see if we had the word *sucker* etched into our foreheads, but it must have been one of those flashing varieties which only lit up when I wasn't looking.

To say that we spent a fair bit of our time at the Theatre Club would be an understatement.

3
A Change at the Top

On returning from our UK trip and much to our dismay we found that Ziggy's boss Doug and his lovely wife Molly would shortly be leaving us. The company's Group had offered Doug a new posting to another country. We were very sad to see them go, Molly had been a pillar of strength for me when we arrived in Zambia, and a good friend.

Shortly before they left they invited Ziggy and me to join them for supper and to meet the new boss Trevor and his wife, Fay. They were originally from London and Fay still had quite a strong cockney accent. They seemed a nice enough couple and I promised Molly that, as far as my relatively limited knowledge would allow, I would give Fay the same support Molly had shown me when we first arrived.

I took Fay on a tour of the various shops and within a week managed to get her a box of butter, some flour and various other rare bits and pieces. During a conversation we'd had at the supper, Fay expressed an interest in joining the Theatre Club, helping backstage. I took her along there one day to introduce her to some of the people and organise her provisional membership.

All new theatre members were given three months in which to prove themselves and we agreed that Fay would help out with some scenery painting for the (then upcoming) *Mary Stuart* play though this wouldn't happen until after the *Old Time Music Hall* had finished its run.

The last night of the *Old Time Music Hall* was the theatre's own Gala Night, which was always particularly special so I got us four tickets. It was an excellent show and we all agreed to stay on for the disco which followed.

That was one *big* mistake.

I won't go into the gory details but suffice it to say that someone upset Fay with a very trivial remark when we sat dangling our feet in the pool. Not only did she get involved in quite a lengthy fracas with a few people sitting nearby, but she actually struck some poor woman which I found out later gave her a black eye! After numerous official complaints were made to the NKAS Committee, they decided it was so serious that Fay had her membership of the Theatre Club revoked.

Trevor's reaction to the pool incident was surprisingly (and disgustingly, I felt) blasé. And not to be outdone by the NKAS committee, the next day he sent out an internal memo at Rhinestone, a copy of which was pasted on the theatre's Notice Board for all to admire.

"To All Employees,

Due to the current financial circumstances of Rhinestone, no further help can be offered to local clubs without the express permission of the Managing Director."

R.I.P. was the response added by one local wit.

I later found out that it was Ziggy who had displayed the memo (and was also the 'local wit' who added the RIP). Naturally he ignored the directive, and continued to supply labour and materials to the Club in his virtually independent position at Rhinestone.

This was all very well, but then I was in a quandary. We had been invited out for supper by Trevor shortly after this event. I had no wish to spend more time in their company and, if forced to, could not trust myself to keep quiet about the state of affairs.

The way I read it, if I did anything to personally upset Fay there was every likelihood that she would try to persuade Trevor to give Ziggy a hard time. I certainly didn't want to risk that.

In the event I phoned and made our apologies, saying I was up to my eyeballs in sewing which had to be completed for the rapidly approaching pantomime (this was actually no lie).

I believe that over the months that followed our esteemed lady-MD attempted a 'Charm Offensive' on other Rhinestone wives, but with little success. I have no idea if she ever did make any actual friends.

* * * * *

In no time at all Christmas was on the doorstep. And with Christmas came Doris, my grandmother. I should perhaps explain that relationships in our family were very casual, and I would often refer to my parents, Nancy and Mev, and my grandmother, Doris, by their first names. Neither were my uncles or aunts actually addressed by that handle, apart from a couple of quite 'great' ones, Uncle Tom and Aunty Ena.

Aunty Ena actually deserves a special mention. She was the official 'Storyteller' on Doris's side of the family. Every alternate Thursday, the 'elderlies' would gather at Tom and Ena's house where my mum and Doris would take along my latest *Dear All* letters.

Once a glass of sherry had been dispensed to all attendees by Uncle Tom, Aunty Ena would put on her spectacles and read out my letters. Apparently she had a knack of perfectly capturing my mannerisms and accent when narrating.

I found this quite amazing, as Aunty Ena was in fact a retired school headmistress, who spoke perfect Queen's English. I, on the other hand, still spoke with a very broad Burtonian accent, which is often mistaken for one coming from 'up north'. Aunty Ena was clearly a lady with very diverse talents.

Anyway, where was I? Oh yes, Doris and Christmas.

Doris had first visited us back in April that year and had so enjoyed it that she 'booked herself in' for another visit, but this time staying for three months, being the maximum time allowed on an economy ticket.

She arrived on Thursday the 10th December. Unfortunately her suitcase didn't. We weren't sure where it went, but it certainly wasn't on the flight to Lusaka. Enquiries eventually revealed that it was languishing in Heathrow airport and that it would be sent on the next available Zambia Airways flight.

On the Saturday afternoon I had arranged to do some work in the Wardrobe at the theatre. Doris accompanied me and as I packed away the previous production's costumes she ferreted around the rails and racks. She found a dress that fitted her, as well as a pair of leather moccasins, which were a welcome change from the heeled pair of shoes she had been wearing for the past three days. She borrowed these items until her suitcase arrived.

It eventually appeared, amazingly intact, five days later. Ziggy slipped some chap at the airport a couple of *kwacha* (the Zambian currency) so the contents, which included lots of treats and our Christmas presents, were not interfered with, inspected, nor charged duty.

That night we feasted on a large, delicious pork pie which, courtesy of the cold London weather, had survived its extended journey remarkably well. The lashings of Branston Pickle from the jar which had accompanied it went down a treat too.

Doris was often likened to the official English Queen Mother, being very similar in stature and age. She always carried herself very erect and when I was a young kid in the '50s and early '60s she would not be seen out without a hat, complete with matching shoes and gloves.

I was pretty much brought up by Doris, or Nannan as she was called when I was young, as my mum and dad were busy running the grocery business she owned. It was the cause of some embarrassment to me with my cousins, that I was clearly her favourite grandchild. But as we lived together I guess it was a natural outcome.

I was well looked after, and rarely asked for anything, as Doris had an uncanny knack of sussing out what was on my unspoken wish list. But it wasn't all easy going. I had to pull my weight helping in the shop whether it was with re-stocking the shelves or serving customers once I was tall enough to see over the counter.

But our relationship was like the clash of the Titans as we were both very strong willed. She frequently chased me down the side street alongside our shop, armed with a plank of wood (stripped from an orange box) with which to wallop my bottom because I had dared to defy her. But I could always out-run her and by the time I sneaked back home she had invariably forgotten all about our little skirmish. Well, most times anyway.

Once I moved out of her 'control' we got along much better, and once Ziggy and I had the children, they attracted much of her attention.

But that Saturday night she couldn't wait to go back to the Club with me and Ziggy to see the friends she had made earlier in the year. She was given a very warm welcome, one befitting of the Queen Mother. Not only was she surrounded by her old friends, as she slowly downed a few gin and tonics, but was already well embroiled with some of the new ones we had made since her last visit.

Her day was complete when someone pitched up with a guitar and started up a sing-a-long. Doris loved music (as did we) but could not sing for toffee. However, she could hold a very tuneful whistle, for which she was famous amongst her circle of friends and acquaintances back in Burton upon Trent, so she would accompany each tune with gusto.

To finish off the night, Mike Glover, who was a regular party participant as well as being the current chairman of the Club, treated us to a rousing rendition of a local ditty. Written, I'm told, by a guy named George Grafton, it was sung to the tune of *In My Liverpool Home*, which if you don't know it, can be heard on the following link:

https://www.youtube.com/watch?v=3lUl9HaFbN8

and the lyrics went something like this (I think I may have to interpret a few words):

I've lived here in Kitwe for just on a year
I've learnt a new language of which I'm not clear
But I'm losing my Englishness more every day

My WC is now called a PK

Chorus
In my new Kitwe Home
In my new Kitwe Home
If you want to say thank you say sanchu mukwai
If you go to a barbecue call it a braai
All the dogs are called voetsek but heaven knows why
In my new Kitwe home

The mine have me housed down in Nkana West
They say that that area is really the best
You can sleep safely and sound as a log
If your windows are barred and you have a big dog!
Chorus: In my new Kitwe home...etc.

The roads tend to dip a bit now and again
The diversions to Kabwe make eunuchs of men
You can drive without lights, overtake on a hill
And if that doesn't kill you the taxicabs will.
Chorus: In my new Kitwe home… etc

We've done some folk singing as you can now see
And one day we even appeared on TV
We came over badly but tell me who won't
When you are on upside down with the sound back to front
Chorus: In my new Kitwe home… etc

We're in a new country developing fast
Those days of the nasty colonials are past
But if off to London you are wanting to fly
Just sing this with me and we'll both be P.I.ed
Chorus: In my new Kitwe home… etc

So just wear a grin, put a smile on your face
You'll find that our town isn't such a bad place
Come down to the theatre if you want to see life
But remember to keep both your eyes on your wife!

Chorus: In my new Kitwe home... etc

(*PK* is too rude to literally interpret but roughly means 'toilet shed'.

Braai (rhymes with 'why') is a South African word for barbecue.

Voetsek (pronounced 'footsack') is an impolite form in Afrikaans for 'go away'.

P.I = Prohibited Immigrant status)

4
Victoria Falls – both of them!

As a result of talking to some of her new friends in the Club, Doris decided she wanted to go to Victoria Falls. As far as most people were concerned it was the only thing (besides copper) that Zambia was famous for, and she had been told that the Falls really were a 'must see'.

The initial plan was for all of us to fly there via Lusaka and Salisbury (Harare), but that was knocked on the head very quickly when we realised the fares alone were going to cost us over £1000 (US$1400), plus hotel accommodation at £400 (US$560), excluding meals. This, I can assure you, was an absolute fortune in those days.

After dallying on the subject for a while, Ziggy came up with the brilliant idea of driving down. Two days driving down, another two coming back, with a week in the middle, staying at all the best hotels, would cost us half as much as flying down. Plans were going along nicely until Ziggy found that a previously booked seven-day holiday by his 2nd-in-command was going to get in the way. The trip had to be delayed, taking us perilously close to Doris's departure date. But we could just squeeze it in.

Then Ziggy discovered that his 2nd-i-c's holiday consisted of seven working days, which messed up the timing completely. It looked like we weren't going to make Victoria Falls before Doris flew home. As soon as she heard this latest development Doris flipped her lid. She flipped it to the degree where she barely avoided being put on the first available flight back to the UK there and then.

Fortunately, after everyone had calmed down, a solution was found. Just Doris and I would fly down to Livingstone for a few days. A trip to the travel agents found the best I could get at such short notice was a flight to Lusaka on Wednesday night, then the second leg on to Livingston on Thursday morning. Our return flight was direct back to Kitwe on Saturday. Some days later Doris and I were having coffee with friends, and I mentioned the trip.

"Oh, don't go paying for accommodation in Lusaka," one of them said. "Blackie Hall is working down Lusaka way for a few weeks and is staying in a 3-bed house by himself. Go and stay with him."

Blackie was another Rhinestone employee who as well as having worked with Ziggy, was a very active member of the Club, and a great guy with a wonderful sense of humour. This suggestion sounded like a fair idea and before I could even ask for his number, someone had called Blackie and arranged it.

Leaving an envious Ziggy and the kids at the airport we flew out of Kitwe the next day. At Lusaka airport we were met by a nice Indian gentleman named Atoke who arrived complete with minibus and driver. I asked him what the plan was.

"Everything is in order Mrs Patras," he explained. "We will now take you to meet up with Blackie at his house in Kafue and he will spend the night with his next-door neighbours. You see, while his house has three bedrooms, it only has one double bed. Not really big enough for all three of you. Ha! Ha! Ha! Ha! Ha!"

I could feel the blood draining from my face. I knew that Kafue was quite some distance from Lusaka, and I also knew there was *no way* I could share a bedroom, never mind a bed, with my grandmother, as she had won the national championships with her record-breaking snoring.

I did my best to persuade Atoke to take us to a hotel instead, but he insisted it was no trouble at all to take us to Kafue. By the time we arrived there *one-and-a-quarter hours* later, we were bored out of our minds, very bum-sore and gasping for a drink.

We were very warmly welcomed by Blackie, and by Ann and Frank Law, his neighbours. As they showed us to the house we would be sleeping in, I informed them of my perverse enjoyment of sleeping on peoples' sofas and asked if they could supply a blanket. Having dumped our gear we went round to their house and had a great night chatting and drinking. On mention of the return trip to the airport, Blackie consoled us with the fact that, during daylight hours, we would really enjoy the wonderful scenery, as it was quite mountainous and 'not nearly as monotonous as the Copperbelt roads'.

Following a reasonable night's sleep, we shared an early breakfast with Ann and Frank before a timely departure for the airport. Unfortunately things once again were not all clean-cut and crystal clear. In fact it wasn't clear at all. We pulled out of their driveway into the thickest pea-souper fog you can imagine. And it stayed like that until we were half way to Lusaka and well beyond any wonderful scenery.

Luckily things improved after that. The hotel we were booked into at Livingstone, the *Mosi o Tunya InterContinental* was pretty decent, with pleasant grounds and a lovely swimming pool. And it was very close to the falls.

Mosi o Tunya translates to *Smoke that Thunders* (smoke equals mist), and believe me, it did! One could clearly hear it from the hotel, hardly surprising as we had only to walk a hundred or so metres (110 yards) through the grounds to see the falls.

And they were pretty awesome, even though we only saw a small section. We were told that the best views were from the Zimbabwe side which we planned to visit the next day. In the meantime we organised a trip to a nearby small game-park as well as a river cruise.

Apart from seeing a few rhino, which I'd seen before, and some giraffe, which I hadn't, the most excitement we had was getting Doris on and off the river boat with the aid of four strong Zambians and a couple of empty beer crates. My grandmother, you see, was not a small woman and had dodgy legs, so wasn't that steady on her feet at the best of times.

We finished off the day, along with a hoard of other people, enjoying the hotel's barbecue which we washed down with a tasty but excessively over-priced Californian Riesling.

Friday was given over to a trip across the border into Zimbabwe. A seven-thirty alarm call ensured we had time to enjoy a full breakfast before our excursion. We had to walk about five hundred metres to reach the Zambian border post where we completed a whole bunch of forms before being allowed through to the taxi rank.

I asked the driver to take us to the nearest Barclays bank so I could cash a cheque for some Zimbabwe dollars. We crossed over Rainbow Bridge, though couldn't see anything of the falls from inside the taxi, before stopping at the Zimbabwe border post to fill in even more forms.

When I eventually got to the bank I told the teller I wanted to buy Zimbabwe dollars by cashing a British cheque backed with my Barclay's Visa card. I asked him how much he thought I would need to cover a trip over the falls in a light plane, a visit to a crocodile farm, food and drink for the day and all taxi fares to and from everywhere. He thought £50 (US$70) worth should cover it so I wrote out my cheque accordingly.

As we went through all the banking rituals he got as far as writing the last three digits of my card number when he suddenly looked up and uttered a very ominous, "Oh, dear".

What, I wondered, *could be wrong now?*

"Oh dear," he repeated "I'm afraid I can't cash this cheque," then wandered off to a back office.

He returned, handing me my cheque, card and the various documents.

"Oh dear," (I was now getting fed up with hearing that) "I'm afraid I can't do this for you. Your Barclaycard expired last year, in November 1981."

My next remark was about something normally found in sewers and I don't mean rats. I asked if he could telex our bank in the UK to verify that there were sufficient funds to cover the cheque, but apparently the nearest telex machine was in Salisbury and they had 'tremendous trouble getting through on the phone'. I said I'd be prepared to wait and could he direct me to the nearest hotel where we could get a drink, until I realised we had no money to pay for it. Nor the taxi, which was outside with its meter running and Doris rapidly melting on the back seat.

After another stroll to discuss the situation with whoever was in the back office, the teller returned saying they thought it really would be a waste of time as the machines in Salisbury, not to mention those who operated them, worked very slowly. I gave up.

Back at the taxi I explained the problem to Doris and the driver. The expression on the driver's face left me in no doubt that he didn't believe a word I was saying and thought I was simply after getting a free taxi ride. I might be a bit stupid down one side on a Thursday, but I wasn't crazy enough to put myself through three hours of paperwork just so that I could get a free taxi ride over Rainbow Bridge.

I promised I would post £5 ($7 USA) to him once we were back in

Kitwe, an excessive amount even for a return trip and the waiting. For a moment I thought he was going to make us get out and walk back, a near impossible feat for Doris.

"Right then, I'm getting out to walk, and we won't pay the fool anything!" Doris chirped up and the driver backed down.

After completing the formalities once more at the Zimbabwe border, he drove us back to the Zambia border post where we alighted full of enthusiasm at the thought of another hour-plus stint of form filling and waiting. I took details of our reluctant driver's address with a promise to put a fiver in the post to him first thing on Monday morning, which of course I did. We never did hear if he received it though. Most likely not, given the local postal workers' ability to smell out money in envelopes from about 500 paces, which is probably why the driver was so unhappy about the arrangement.

The serving of lunch was almost over by the time we had walked back the final stretch to the hotel, but we managed to glean some scraps off the buffet table. We then spent a very relaxing couple of hours beside (and in) the pool before going to take a more thorough look at the falls.

Doris was content to plonk herself down on a low stone wall at a point where she could see a small section of the cascading water while I continued on. Have you ever walked through a quarter-mile long shower? It's different. I sloshed along the soggy path until I reached the furthest point you can get on the Zambian side. The whole area was unfenced, no barriers, nothing. Just a sheer hundred metre drop into the fast-flowing Zambezi River if you got too close.

Everything, and I mean every single item of clothing I was wearing, got absolutely saturated. But it was worth it. The falls were spectacular. I had taken my camera with me but was afraid to remove it from its pouch in case it was damaged by the very fine mist which accompanied the warm shower. I eventually plucked up the courage to snap a couple of shots when the wind changed and blew the mist away from me.

After about twenty minutes I returned to Doris, looking as if I had gone over the falls instead of viewing them. And boy, it was hot! We took a slow stroll back to the hotel where we returned to the poolside and got wet in a more conventional manner.

That evening we enjoyed another barbecue meal and afterwards sat chatting with a British couple and the hotel chef, who joined us when he had finished his duties. When the couple eventually got up to leave, Doris also decided to retire for the night.

Within half an hour I had been propositioned by the chef!

Naturally I declined his invitation to inspect his living quarters. Not to be deterred he then suggested that we might go skinny dipping in the moonlit pool and whilst I declined that kind offer too, he proceeded to strip. As he paraded by the water's edge, before posing and diving into the pool, I couldn't help but notice that it was highly unlikely he would have been able to reach the standard I was used to, had I accepted his initial invitation.

On our arrival back in Kitwe we were greeted by my beloved husband and three of the filthiest children I had ever seen. In contrast to their mother, I don't think they had been near any water the entire time we had been away.

* * * * *

One day prior to Doris's visit, I had been sitting at the dining table, driving my sewing machine at its maximum speed as per usual. It was the half-term holiday for the kids, who I could hear playing in the front garden. This was always a good sign. It was when I could not hear them that I would worry.

I had finished making one tedious garment and got up to have a good stretch and decided to see if the kids would like a drink. As I walked out to the steps leading from the front door I could only see Brad and Leon playing beneath the flamboyant tree, or the climbing tree as we called it, due to its form which made for easy climbing onto the lower sturdy branches.

"Come and look at this, Leon," called Brad, pointing to something at the base of the tree trunk.

Then I heard Vicki's voice.

"What you found, Brad?"

I froze on the spot at the top of the steps as I realised where Vicki's voice was coming from, and slowly raised my eyes to see her happily stretched out on one of the upper branches of the tree. Before I could move or say a word, she had put out her arm to grasp another branch so she could turn to see what Brad and Leon were looking at. Unfortunately this branch was little more than a twig.

With a faint but decisive 'crack' the twig broke under her slight weight and Vicki plummeted to the ground, landing with a thud just inches away from a small stone wall.

I bounded down the steps to where she lay, fearing the worst, but as I reached her she pushed herself up to a sitting position.

"Ouch! Oh hello mummy," she said with a sheepish, pained grin on her face.

I thoroughly checked her all over and finding no obvious broken bits, lifted her off the ground.

"That was very silly to go so high up into the tree, Vicki," I admonished, "what on earth were you thinking of?"

"I wanted to see what it would look like if I was a bird," she replied.

"Well, at least now you know you can't fly like one," said Brad, as he and Leon fell about giggling. Little sods.

"So where does it hurt?" I asked.

"My foot hurts a bit."

I looked at both feet but nothing appeared broken so I lowered her gently to a standing position on the ground.

"Ow, mummy, this one hurts a bit," she said, pointing to her right foot.

"Okay, kids, let's go," I said, picking up Vicki again.

"Where we going, mummy?" Brad asked.

"To the Company Clinic."

"Oh *no*, not *again!*" groaned Leon in an exasperated voice.

"Oh stop whining, Leon," said Brad.

This was good coming from him, since he had been the cause of our last emergency visit to the clinic.

I sent the boys to get cleaned up while I phoned Ziggy and asked him to send Peter, his driver, to collect us and take us to the clinic. I had time to wash Vicki's hands and face and smarten myself up when Peter arrived.

X-rays revealed that Vicki had suffered greenstick fractures in three bones in her foot. It was an amazing escape, really, considering she must have fallen almost ten feet to the ground. Her ankle and foot were firmly strapped and we were told that she wasn't to put any weight on it for at least two weeks. In any event they wanted to check her progress after a week.

While the nurse was bandaging Vicki's ankle she glanced across at Brad who was on the point of interfering with an oxygen line.

"So how are your fingers now, Brad?" she asked. "All better?"

"Yes, great, thank you," he said, pushing them under her nose so that she could inspect the bright red scars across the underside of three of his fingers.

A few weeks earlier, on our way to the Club for an afternoon of swimming, we had first called at a curtain fabric shop in town. I needed to buy additional material to make a dress for Queen Elizabeth, a character in the *Mary Stuart* play. I found the perfect fabric in a roll of gold brocade and asked the assistant to measure and cut three metres for me.

Being October it was a very hot day and the shop had a stand-fan vainly attempting to replicate a cooling breeze. The fan was very noisy, at one point emitting an odd 'kerdunking' noise. The assistant had almost finished folding the cloth and looked up, past me and screamed. I quickly turned to see if there was a panga-wielding maniac walking through the door and instead saw

Brad, hands cupped in front of him, with blood dripping profusely into a puddle on the floor.

"Oh, my God!"

It only took me a couple of seconds to put two and two together and deduce that the little boy's fingers had been sliced by fan blades.

"Give me some scrap material, quick!" I demanded of the assistant.

She rummaged through a nearby box and passed me a wad of material and some thin strips of lining. I quickly opened Brad's hand, curved his fingers round the wad of material and bandaged it tight with the strips. We were only a street away from the Company Clinic so we raced round there on foot, where I briefly explained to the nurse what had happened.

"So, Brad, what have you done *this* time?" she said, looking him in the eye.

"Well, I was bored, and this fan was making a terrible racket, so I thought I'd see if I could stop it doing that."

"So you put your fingers inside the fan guard to stop it?"

"Yes. But then it made a worse noise, so I pulled 'em out. My fingers didn't hurt that much to start with, and when I first looked at them they weren't bleeding. But then they just did, I suppose."

"Okay, then, let's have a look."

She slowly unwound the emergency bandage and then, keeping Brad's fingers curled, carefully removed the wad of fabric. She expressed delight that the bleeding had stopped and the cuts had stayed closed, thanks, she said, to my quick and deft first aid measures. (It is amazing the skills one acquires as one becomes a mother.)

It took a while but she managed to clean the blood from his fingers and hand without the wounds opening. Then she expertly applied thin strips of micropore tape (I'd never heard of this before) in a criss-cross pattern over the cuts. To minimise the risk of strain on the cuts, she re-bandaged his hand with his fingers still curled. We were told to attend the clinic daily to have the wounds re-dressed.

We returned to the curtain shop, where the assistant had barely recovered from mopping up the bloody puddle, to pay for and collect the material. Then we resumed our shopping trip before going to the Club. Of course Brad went round showing everyone his bandaged hand, regaling them with the full gory details, and wallowing in the praise at how brave he'd been not to cry when it happened. However, the smile soon disappeared from his face when he was told that he wasn't allowed to swim before his hand had completely healed.

But back to Vicki.

Once we'd sorted her out at the clinic I got Peter to drop us at the Club as it wouldn't be long before Ziggy would be making his way there after work. Like Brad, Vicki wanted to 'show off' her injury to her friends. And, like Brad, it didn't take her long to discover that being injured had its disadvantages.

Being unable to walk was highly inconvenient when it came to playing with her friends.

The option of using crutches was completely out of the question for one so young and small. As Vicki sat on the grass, watching the other kids run around and play on the swings, we racked our brains to think of a way of mobilising her.

"It's a pity we don't still have the twin pushchair," I observed, "at least everyone would have been able to move her around more easily on wheels."

A couple of minutes later Ziggy said, "I've got it! I know exactly what will sort her out."

He obviously wasn't going to share his stroke of genius with me so I ordered another drink and went to talk to a friend, leaving Ziggy to huddle over his notebook, secretly drawing something.

The next day Ziggy returned home from work, walking in with a big grin on his face.

"I want everyone to go into the lounge and close your eyes," he said.

Knowing questions would get us nowhere, we did as we were bid.

Shortly afterwards we heard a strange scuttling noise.

"Okay, you can look now."

We opened our eyes to see a strange object moving along the floor. It looked like a little foot-stool on wheels.

"This is for Vicki," he proudly announced. Brad immediately made a dive for it.

"Oh no you don't!" admonished Ziggy, "I said it was for *Vicki*, and that's what I meant. It is not for you boys to play on."

Then he went over to where Vicki was sitting wide-eyed, picked her up and plonked her down on the one-foot-square seat. He told her to hold onto the sides with her hands then said,

"Go on then, kick yourself along with your good foot."

With her right leg stuck out in front of her, she gave a big push on the floor with her left foot.

"Yayyyyy!" she screamed, laughing fit to burst with excitement, as she shot backwards at a great rate of knots, straight out the door before crashing into the passage wall. It's the biggest wonder she wasn't thrown to the floor with the force of it. The boys were jumping up and down equally excited, very, very envious of their 'lucky' sister.

Whilst I was thrilled to bits for Vicki, I was also filled with trepidation at the thought of what damage might be caused to other legs, human, animal or wooden, during the lifetime of this mobility contraption. And that was before envisaging what could happen when the boys eventually got their hands on it (especially Brad, the family's unofficial wrecker and demolition expert).

When the kids returned to school the following week, the staff at the Round Table had mixed feelings about Vicki's mode of transport. Whilst they were delighted for her being independently mobile, they were not so enamoured with the distraction it created in the classroom. Vicki soon found herself with even more friends than usual during playtime, as they queued up to take turns 'riding the stool'.

"You can have a go on it," she would tell them "so long as you don't crash it, and only for the time it takes for me to count up to number twenty."

Had that been Brad, I'm sure he would have been selling 'rides for sweets'.

Miraculously Ziggy's wonderful invention managed to stay in one piece for as long as Vicki needed to use it, after which it reverted to a normal little footstool, the wheels being removed for safety's and everyone else's sake.

5

A Trip to Chingola

One weekend Benton had to go to Chingola for some important church event.

I needed to go into Chingola (a town some thirty miles away) myself to borrow some costumes from CAS (Chingola Arts Society) which were needed for a production in which I was involved, so I offered to give him a lift back home on the Monday morning. I arranged to meet him at a well-known junction near the bus depot at ten o'clock.

The kids were on school holidays at the time and as Benton naturally wasn't at home to look after them for me, I had to take them with me; not a prospect I relished on such a tedious journey I can tell you. They were supplied with books for the journey, some for reading and some for colouring, and I hoped they respected the difference.

I had met up with the Chingola wardrobe mistress early as she needed to dash off to work and then I picked up Benton at the duly appointed place. As we were exiting the town centre, Benton hastily begged a favour for which he apologised in advance. Could we please give a lift to his cousin who was also leaving Chingola? Before I had a chance to consider his request I nearly jumped out of my skin.

"There he is, Madam!" he shouted in my ear, his arm shooting across the steering wheel to point at someone waiting at a petrol station.

As I slowed to a halt, Benton leapt out of the car and ran across the road to his cousin. After a couple of minutes jabbering to each other, and gesticulating in various directions, the two hastened back across the road. It was only then that I noticed Benton's cousin had a wooden leg.

At this point I should mention that we had been having trouble with the door behind the driver's seat, insofar as it was extremely difficult to open. Benton led the hobbling cousin round to the passenger side of the vehicle from where he introduced him to me.

"Madam, this is Fountain. Fountain this is Madam."

Fountain put his hands together in a small clapping gesture, making a slight bow as is the African greeting custom, and thanked me profusely for my kind generosity in helping him to his destination. Benton then opened the rear door for his relative to climb in beside my kids.

There was obviously some hierarchy at play here, as it would obviously have been much easier if Benton had taken the back seat and allowed the disabled Fountain to sit in the front.

Even in those days, when most folk in Zambia apparently had no idea about the purpose of seat-belts, Ziggy and I had been very strict on the wearing of them. All three of my kids were already strapped in, Brad on the left, Vicki in the centre spot and Leon behind me on the right. After much juggling around, Benton managed to fasten both Vicki and Leon into the centre position, thus making space for Fountain on the right.

Clutching a large, ball-shaped cloth parcel as if it contained his life's possessions (it probably did) and a homemade bamboo crutch, Fountain battled his way into the seat behind me. (Vehicles in Zambia were right-hand drive, like in the UK.) This manoeuvre was not a simple process as Fountain was surprisingly tall for a Zambian, much taller than Benton, who only reached five feet two inches on a generous day.

As he clambered across the kids, his prosthetic limb narrowly missed going in my ear and, as it swung backwards, would have parted Benton's hair clean down the middle had it not been so short (Benton's hair, not the wooden leg). Having come into close proximity with this unusual appendage I wondered how he had come to lose half his leg in the first place, as the limb extension he now possessed looked as if it had been gnawed on by a hyena.

Once he was settled in his seat I resumed our journey; the two Africans prattled away in their own language while the kids sat quietly, their eyes riveted on the mysterious impressions visible on the piece of wood projecting from the bottom of Fountain's rather short trouser leg.

As I drove on I couldn't help wondering about our new passenger's name.

Before we go any further, dear reader, let me quote to you a few passages from my first epistle, *Into Africa*, which may explain the previous statement.

I could not understand why the Zambian people have such peculiar names, and we ARE talking first names here, first names which sound more like English surnames. I would have expected more traditional African names.

When I asked the question of one of the older expatriates she said that years ago the servants would often name their children after the surname of their employer. I could go with that up to a point,

"But what happened if they had more than one child?" I asked. "From what I've heard, some houseboys stay with a family for decades. And from what I've seen they have loads of kids too. They can't call them all by the same (sur)name!"

"No," she replied, "then they find something else, like the farm tractor or the bwana's car."

I thought, 'there must be a helluva lot of Masseys, Fergusons, John Deeres and Fords around'.

"OR," she'd continued, "the mother may name the baby after an event or a feeling, or even something she saw around the time of the birth."

I didn't know how true any of this was, but it seemed to make a modicum of sense to me at the time.

But back to this story…

As I drove, and despite giving the subject considerable thought, I could not imagine what colonial architectural delight his mother or father must have seen before he was born to warrant my new passenger being endowed with such a moniker as Fountain. I certainly couldn't recall seeing anything resembling a fountain on my travels thus far in Zambia.

The journey continued uneventfully until we reached a long bend in the road. I might have avoided an enormous pothole on my side of the road, were it not for a huge mine truck hurtling towards us. Being unable to completely avoid the pothole, my left wheel caught the edge of the pit and created a bounce so ferocious that it almost sent Fountain up through the roof.

I was marvelling at the fact that the car still seemed to be travelling on four round wheels when Fountain began shouting in the back and Benton instructed me to stop the car pretty damn quick.

Before I had even managed to grind to a halt, Fountain, clutching his package in one arm and waving his crutch with the other, had somehow succeeded in opening the defective rear door and could be seen hotfoot-and-stumping it into the bundu (South African term for 'the bush') faster than I would have thought possible.

Silence reigned for a few moments whilst we recovered from this unexpected and hasty departure, before continuing yet again on our journey.

We hadn't gone very far when I heard this strange 'ump-ump'ing noise. I glanced over my shoulder and caught sight of Brad, his lips pursed, his cheeks puffed out, and his eyes wild.

"Ump, ump…"

He was obviously going to be sick.

Leon and Vicki then began yelling, "Mummy! Mummy! Mummy!"

I thought it was at Brad's predicament. Craning my head over my shoulder, whilst still trying to watch the road, I turned to ascertain what the commotion was all about.

Before I could say or do a thing, Brad had barfed down the back of Benton's seat. Vicki and Leon were screaming and trying to escape from their tethered positions, stuck between Brad on their left, and on their right by something I had now identified by sight and smell. This was the cue for me to start retching from the depths of my stomach.

The reason for Fountain's hasty departure was now all too apparent. The shock of the oncoming truck and his near projection through the roof was too much for him and he had shat himself. The evidence of this was now seeping across the back seat of the car towards the kids.

As the car skidded to a halt in a cloud of grit and dust by the side of the road, Benton and I simultaneously sprang from the vehicle and extricated the kids from the stinking mobile toilet.

We moved away to a safe breathing distance where Brad continued to barf and I continued to heave, whilst Vicki and Leon clung to my legs like bear cubs up a tree, still shaking and crying their little hearts out. Benton had disappeared completely.

It must have been at least five minutes before everyone calmed down and regrouped. Poor Benton was mortified.

"Sorry Madam. Sorry Madam. Oh sorry, sorry, sorry. I am so sorry, Madam, for what my cousin did. Sorry, sorry, sorry."

Not half as sorry as you're going to be, I thought, *because someone has to clear this mess up before we can continue our journey, and it sure as shit isn't going to be me!*

Fortunately, and appropriate for reasons I had never before considered coming into play, we carried a 2-litre plastic container of water in the boot. In an 'Emergencies Box' we kept there too, there was a toilet roll, an empty plastic bag for rubbish, and an old towel.

I took the kids for a nature ramble into the *bundu*, hoping we wouldn't meet any snakes or lions along the way, leaving Benton to clean up.

Given the limited equipment available he did a pretty good job but even leaving the doors open throughout, the lack of any breeze whatsoever meant the overbearing stink still hovered. And then he needed to clean himself up.

I hadn't noticed upon exiting the car exactly how much regurgitated breakfast Brad had managed to share with Benton, or the back of his shirt to be more precise. The poor man had tried to clean it up but with no water left in the container, it ended up looking worse than ever. I ferreted about in the boot of the car and amongst the items I had borrowed from CAS was a blouse (not *too* frilly) which I handed to Benton for him to change into.

Returning from his temporary change-room behind some bushes, we eventually bit the bullet and retook our seats, although I had a hell of a job persuading the kids to sit in the back. They all wanted the front seat.

After quite a long period of silence I broke the ice by asking Benton where his cousin lived, since his rapid departure had occurred in what appeared to be the middle of nowhere; though you would be surprised where people suddenly appear from on these long, seemingly uninhabited stretches of nothingness in Africa.

"I don't know," he said.

"What do you mean, 'you don't know'? He is your cousin, isn't he?"

"Yes, Madam, but he is not a very well-known cousin."

"What do you mean?"

"He is the husband of my mother's father's brother's daughter," he replied, as if that explained everything.

If that were me I would simply have said he was married to my second cousin, or was my great-uncle's son-in-law, but in Africa they had a totally different set-up to us.

I never did figure it out completely, but they did not refer to in-laws like we do. And uncles and aunts only apply when the descending sex is different, otherwise your father's brother is also your father, as your mother's sister is also your mother, whereas your father's sister isn't your mother, she's your aunt, but your mother's mother's sister can be your grandmother, and so on.

This explains why Zambians take so much time off work to go to their grandfather's funeral, who had already died six months ago, and the year before that too.

We eventually arrived home and went rapidly inside to get everyone showered and changed. I left the car with Benton for a more thorough clean before Ziggy reclaimed it. I tried desperately not to laugh as I handed him the car keys. He looked ever so sweet in the bright blue and red flowery blouse he was wearing.

I somehow didn't think he'd be asking me for lifts again any time soon.

6
Holiday of a Lifetime

When I was first thinking of using chapter headings in this book, I thought this one would have been called 'How not to take a holiday'. But it was by no means the worst holiday I've ever had, possibly just one of the most memorable.

As we reached the middle of March 1982, Ziggy announced that his work schedule was looking incredibly tidy, and that before the commencement of the next stage of his current project, he could take a few days off. On the Sunday night before Vicki and Leon's birthday he suggested that we could perhaps go to Livingstone (following my wonderful report on Victoria Falls) for a few days and asked me to book it.

So on Monday morning I did.

When he came home for lunch he announced he'd changed his mind and wanted to fly to Zimbabwe instead, as he had discovered that if he said he was going on business, we could get a foreign exchange allowance without having to draw on our UK based money. He asked me to change the destination, and to make it for a week. So I did.

Did you notice how easily those sentences and paragraphs flowed across the paper? Obviously because writing it was so easy. Doing it was not. Making hotel bookings was no simple task. Booking seats on flights through travel agents whose phones don't work, and neither did most of the staff, was a painfully exhausting, frustrating and lengthy experience.

But that was okay, I hadn't had much to do apart from make two finicky dresses for an old lady and finish making a *silk* shirt for a man who was leaving on an overseas trip. (My association with the Theatre filled my spare (?!) time with a great many personal requests for dressmaking.)

Making a load of new clothes for Vicki and Leon, whose fourth birthday was on the Tuesday, buying and putting together little gift parcels for all the guests, and making four birthday cakes (two for school and two for home) didn't count. Those chores weren't considered *real* work.

At the end of the busy Tuesday morning I was finishing off the food preparations for the party when the phone rang. It was Ziggy. He doesn't like to 'waste time' on the telephone, so this was not a good sign.

"Change the flights!"

"What?"

"I want you to go and change the flights."

"Why?"

"I want to go to Durban instead."

"Why?"

"My new mate George came into the office. He got back from there last night and was raving about it, said he had a fantastic holiday. Then Simon dropped in and heard us talking about it and said he'd been there the week before, and he'd had a great time too. So I want you to go right now and change our flights to Durban."

"What, as in Durban, South Africa?"

"Yes. Go on, do it now."

"But I'm in the middle of ... I've got the kids party in ..."

"You have to do it straight away or we won't get tickets, because I want you to book it to include the Easter weekend, then we can go for eleven days," and he was gone.

I finished chipping the potatoes I had been preparing and put sausages into a roasting pan to cook slowly in the oven before optimistically heading for the telephone. I should have known better. There was no reply from Best Travel. Knowing that the only way to really do business in this country was face to face, I grabbed my handbag and dashed off to town. Luckily I had the company car that day.

The travel agent I had dealt with before was not amused when I told her I wanted to make changes to our itinerary, saying she was very busy and couldn't possibly deal with it until the next day. Fortunately one of her colleagues took pity on me and offered to do whatever she could. What a nice lady Wendy was.

I told her where we wanted to go, and it needed to include Easter. She checked through available flights. She said there was a good connection down to Durban on the Friday of the following week so we agreed that she should 'go for that'.

Unfortunately any bookings with Zambia Airways for more than four people had to be confirmed by their Lusaka office. Getting through to the Lusaka office was a nightmare. However using two telephones, and a lot of perseverance, Wendy eventually managed to reach them.

Zambia Airways staff members were not known for their speed and efficiency, and when Wendy was told that they would call her back with confirmation, we knew we could be in for quite a wait. The previous fifteen minutes hanging onto telephones had given us time for a good chat, so she was fully aware of my rather hectic schedule and suggested that I leave it in her capable hands. She would call me the instant she had any news.

"Don't forget to check that all your vaccinations are up to date before you go," Wendy called, as I was half way out the door, "or they won't let you back into the country on your return."

I arrived home just as Brad, Vicki and Leon were being dropped off from school. We had an hour to complete preparations before a swarm of excited little party people arrived.

What a wonderful time was had by the twenty screaming kids, racing around, playing games and spilling drinks and food down their nice party clothes. The sausages and chips, served in brown-paper cones, with lashings of ketchup, went down a treat, as did the jelly and cake after two choruses of

Happy Birthday and the blowing out of candles.

Later that night I filled Ziggy in on the day's events. Wendy had phoned me before five o'clock, confirming that we could fly out on Friday the following week, returning on Easter Monday.

Preparations for our departure were considerable although one thing that didn't take long was packing. Going to South Africa was like going to the UK. You went with near-empty suitcases, did a whole load of shopping and returned with full ones. Whilst we were taking five suitcases, two of the kids' cases would easily fit inside ours, even with sufficient clothes to keep us all going until we could get to the shops.

"I am so looking forward to this break," said Ziggy. "An injection of relaxation is exactly what I need right now."

"Oh, thank heaven you said that."

"Said what?"

"Injection. We need to make sure our vaccinations are up to date. Where are the certificates?"

"With the passports. And before you ask … I'll get them."

It was a good job we checked. Our cholera certificates were two months out of date. We went along to the government clinic first thing the next morning and had them done. What a performance that was. As a result the kids were two hours late getting to school.

During the week that followed we were chatting to folk at the Club and discovered that eight others were flying to South Africa on the same day. Their flight was at 7am out of Kitwe, and they took great delight in ribbing us when they heard that ours was out of Ndola, an hour's drive away.

Departure day soon arrived and we were up at some ungodly hour in the morning to arrive at Ndola for our 7am flight. When we stepped out onto the airport's apron we were delighted to be greeted by a spit-spanking, brand-new jet aircraft. What a pleasure. The coffee and biscuits service from the hostesses was excellent too and they had to be quick as the flight landed well within the hour. I say 'coffee and biscuits' but Ziggy asked for a beer.

"Start your holiday as you mean to go on, I always say," was his motto.

As we strolled through the arrivals hall we realised that our compatriots were still making their way from Kitwe in an old propeller driven plane. We took great delight in lining up outside arrivals when they landed half an hour later.

"Welcome to Lusaka guys. What kept you?"

Their faces were a picture!

The flight to Johannesburg was due to leave at 9:00 but at 8:45 there were still 6000 people (or so it seemed) waiting to go through passport control. Only at 8:50 did they decide to put a second official on passport duty, and we eventually made it through to the sole departure lounge.

There was no such thing as seat reservation back then and I was, of course, anxious that the five of us should be able to sit together. Seeing people going through the departures gate, I approached one of the ground staff and asked her if she could possibly call passengers with small children on our flight to go through first. She said she would. Her colleague, standing by the door, looked at her watch, then looked around at the accumulating passengers.

"Are there any more passengers for the Nairobi flight?" she said.

No-one appeared to take any notice of her, but at least it explained why so many people had been filtering out.

After about ten minutes the gate light began to flash.

"Are there any more passengers for the Nairobi flight?" the woman shouted.

At this, a bloke who had actually come through passport control at the same time as we did (I recognised him because he was wearing an incredibly garish tie) went over to her and presenting his boarding pass. After a few utterances he shot off through the door, followed fifteen seconds later by another gentleman.

By the time I made it back to the huge plate glass window, where Ziggy and the kids stood, the steps for one aircraft had been hauled away and the plane began its push-back on the apron. Then I saw the tie man. He shot out of the building like someone had shoved a rocket up his backside.

"Wait for me! Wait for me!" he shouted, waving his ticket in the air with one hand, his briefcase in the other as he tore across the concrete.

He'd got about half way to the slowly reversing plane when he must have tripped over his own feet. With both hands otherwise occupied, the poor man didn't stand a chance and landed flat on his face. By this time the majority of the remaining passengers in the lounge had moved to the windows to see what our crowd had been yelling about. As the guy hit the deck a collective cry of, *Oooo, Ouch* went up.

After what seemed like ages of immobility he began to lift himself up. He was joined by the other gentleman, clearly not as fit as he was, but who tried to help him, at the same time taking up the cry for the plane to wait.

The driver of the tractor pushing the plane stopped, then climbed down to talk to the driver of the tractor which had removed the steps. Then both tractor drivers and the two (hopeful) passengers were conducting a semaphoric conversation with the pilot of the plane, who was gesticulating from the other side of the cockpit window. This ensued for several minutes.

Then the plane's door began to open and the stairs were guided back into place. As the two men hobbled up the flight of steps an enormous cheer and round of applause went up inside the departure lounge with shouts of *Hurray! Yay! Woohoo!* as the two disappeared inside the plane and the door closed behind them.

Everyone settled back in their previous positions to await the call for our departure. A buzz was going round the room that the reason for our delay was that the Zambia Airways plane which should have been winging us to Johannesburg had been grounded as being 'unsafe'. They had arranged to borrow another aircraft from somewhere. We were delighted to find that they had borrowed a British Airways 707, complete with BA flight and cabin crew.

When the flight was called, our friends, Karin and Tom Stalker with their two boys, and us with our three kids, managed to get ahead of the crowd and secure seats for us all (including the four other Kitweans) at the rear of the aircraft. Everyone was seated and raring to get on with their journey when one of the BA hostesses came walking down the aisle to talk to her colleague in the rear galley.

"You'll never guess what the airport idiots have done now," she said in hushed tones. "They've only gone and put all the food for our first class passengers on the flight that's just left for Nairobi!"

Well, I curled up. My pals had been talking amongst themselves and hadn't heard this so wanted to know what the hell I was laughing at. When I told them they all began hooting and howling like a load of lunatics.

After a few minutes the Captain made an announcement.

"Ladies and gentlemen, our apologies for the delay. The cabin crew will shortly be bringing round warm, but at least wet, Coca Cola's for your enjoyment. Unfortunately Lusaka Airport seem unable to provide cold ones or ice."

He went on.

"I regret to advise that the reason for this is that there will be a further short delay due to the fact that we are having to wait for additional catering facilities for our flight."

Of course, the back of the plane erupted into howling laughter again. We eventually took off at about 10:10. By this time we were getting on famously with the British Airways hostesses who, I think, were happy that someone could see the funny side of all the problems. When we landed there was yet another delay. We were rather puzzled when the cabin crew walked down the aisle handing out wads of paper napkins. Then the Captain spoke.

"Ladies and gentlemen, I would ask you to please all remain in your seats as we have yet another problem to resolve, courtesy of the Zambia Airport Authorities. Your patience is greatly appreciated."

Apparently South Africa was not affected by malaria, so any planes coming into the country from malaria-riddled regions had to be sprayed to kill off any malaria carrying mozzies which might have buzzed into the plane whilst it was on the ground. Normally the plane interiors are sprayed before passengers board but Lusaka airport, in its usual inefficient way, had managed to run out of the appropriate pesticide.

We had to wait for a Johannesburg ground crew member to pass cans of spray through a barely opened door. These were then carried by cabin crew who, holding wads of napkins to their own faces, and indicated that we should do the same, began to spray a thick cloud of deadly fumes above our heads for the length of the plane. Then we had to remain in our seats for fifteen minutes whilst the stuff took effect.

What, at the time of booking, had seemed like quite a long stopover in Johannesburg, now gave us only enough time to transfer to our final flight to Durban. We bade farewells and 'happy holidays' to our friends who were remaining in Johannesburg and made our way to another terminal for our final flight.

That leg of our journey went completely unhindered as we enjoyed our first ever flight on an Airbus. The South African Airways crew were friendly and efficient and the Captain kept us updated on our progress, as well as that of a cricket test match currently being played down in Cape Town.

"But for those of you flying with us today who are unfamiliar with the wonderful game of cricket," he said, "I shall explain."

This was his explanation...

"You have two sides, one out in the field and one in.

Each man that's in the side that's in goes out, and when he's out he comes in and the next man goes in until he's out.

When they are all out, the side that's out comes in and the side that's been in goes out and tries to get those coming in, out.

Sometimes you get men still in and not out.

When a man goes out to go in, the men who are out try to get him out, and when he is out he goes in and the next man in goes out and goes in.

There are two men called umpires who stay out all the time and they decide when the men who are in are out.

When both sides have been in and all the men are out, and both sides have been out twice after all the men have been in, including those who are not out, that is the end of the game!

Howzat!"

A wave of laughter and applause went around the plane. We thought it was brilliant. We'd never experienced anything this laid-back before.

* * * * *

When I had collected the tickets from Best Travel, Wendy tried to book us into the Malibou Hotel on Durban's seafront, but alas, their telex machine appeared not to be working, so we decided to take our chances on being able to book in when we arrived.

In the event, once we'd loaded ourselves and our baggage into a taxi, Ziggy asked the driver to take us to the Hoffman Seaboard. I peered at my husband.

"This is where George and his family stayed. He reckons it's a great place so I thought we'd try it for one night, and next day look at the Malibou and then decide where we want to spend the other nine days."

I couldn't argue with that. So we poured out of the taxi and into the Hoffman Seaboard Hotel and Apartments reception. As I stood with the kids guarding our possessions (old habits die hard) Ziggy approached the large reception desk, manned by a rather pretty young lady bearing a name badge on her very ample left appendage. Her right one was fairly ample too.

Ziggy stared at the badge (yeah, right!) as if he had a reading disability, before eventually dragging his eyes towards her face.

"Hello, er, Gloria," he said, glancing back at the badge, before looking up again, beaming like a Cheshire cat.

"Good afternoon, Sir, welcome to the Hoffman Seaboard. How can I help you?" she asked, returning his smile.

You really don't want him to answer that honestly, I thought.

"I wonder if you have space for me and my family in your establishment," he said.

"Oh, I'm sure we can fit you in," she beamed. "How long would you like to stay?"

"Just for the one night, to start with. Then we may stay for another nine days, if we like it."

"I can give you one of our nicest apartments, and I'm sure you will love it here," Gloria said sweetly, pulling back her shoulders. "Are you sure I can't book you in for the entire duration?"

"Well, since you've made such an offer, how can I refuse?" he replied, battling to take his eyes away from her prize features.

I couldn't believe my ears. What a pushover he was.

"And how will you be paying, Sir?"

"American Express."

I waited for the classic response (*that'll do nicely*) but was disappointed.

"Shall I take for the entire stay, Sir?" she said instead.

"Yes, why not?"

I was livid.

How could he do this? All on the strength of a large pair of boobs?

When he'd finished signing away half our year's savings to the voluptuous Gloria, she handed over the key to the apartment and we headed for the lift, followed by an aging black porter who had suddenly materialised from nowhere to take our bags.

Of course, Ziggy didn't notice the silent treatment he was getting as we rode up in the lift, or when the kids raced ahead to find Apartment 274.

Ziggy unlocked the door and ceremoniously ushered me in first. I couldn't believe my eyes. I entered through the kitchenette and looked through the open-plan arrangement to the lounge which lay beyond, and was horrified to see a large open window.

The kids rushed in past me, heading for the sofa on which to climb to look at the view through the window. Luckily I managed to get there first and slide the glass closed, securing it shut with a simple latch mechanism. Despite the heat I went cold at the thought of the potential danger that window presented if we turned our backs for a moment.

We were on the 27th floor!

We explored the apartment in the space of ten seconds flat. There was a small bathroom and beyond the double bedroom a curtained extension contained two narrow single beds.

"I thought your friend Gloria said she had a six bed apartment," I said to Ziggy, and seeing the telephone, "I think you'd better tell her she gave us the wrong keys."

Ziggy got on the phone immediately and explained the error. I waited impatiently as he listened to her reply. Putting down the phone, he turned to me.

"It would seem this *is* a six-bed apartment. Apparently the sofa in the lounge opens out to make a double bed."

"That sofa the kids can climb on, and open the windows? Terrific!"

I was not a happy lady. I plonked myself down on the sofa bed and seethed. After a few minutes I realised the futility of this practice and began to unpack our few things into the wardrobe, toiletries into the bathroom and other such mundane actions.

"Let's go and get something to eat," said Ziggy.

That sounded like a good plan to me, so after hands and faces had been washed we went in search of food.

When we entered the reception area it was empty.

"Hello, hello, is there anyone around?"

Ziggy looked over the counter to see if the gorgeous Gloria was perhaps sitting on a low chair having a rest, but it was devoid of all human life.

Again, out of nowhere, appeared the little black porter, but this time he was wearing his doorman's hat.

"Where is Gloria, the receptionist?"

"She is gone."

"Yes, I can see she is gone," Ziggy sighed, "but when will she be back?"

"On Monday, Sir."

"On *Monday*? Then who is in charge here until Monday?"

"I am, Sir," the doorman said, suddenly standing proudly to attention.

"Okay," I enquired of the porter/doorman/person-now-in-charge, "can you tell us what floor the dining room or restaurant is on, please?"

"Ah, Madam, we don't have that."

"What, nothing?"

"No, Madam. The dining room was closed many years ago, Madam."

"Well, what about a bar, where we can perhaps buy some snacks?"

"If you go out of the door and turn right, then walk down as far as ...."

"Isn't there a bar here, in the hotel?" Ziggy asked now.

"No Sir, no bar Sir."

"Then how can you call this place the Hoffman Seaboard *Hotel* and Apartments if there are no hotel facilities?"

"Oh, it has always been called a hotel and apartments, Sir."

We gave up.

"Let's see what we can find on the streets," said Ziggy as I then conjured up a picture of us scratching through the rubbish bins attached to the street lights.

After a short walk we came across a no-name-brand fast food restaurant type place and enjoyed a mediocre meal of burgers and chips with a dessert comprising a pre-wrapped ice-cream of your choice from the freezer cabinet. It was not exactly the culinary treat we had had in mind, but it sufficed.

The kids naturally wanted to see the sea, and as the sun had just set we knew there wouldn't be much daylight left so we hurried along to the beachfront. There weren't many people on the beach, and those who were there, were white. I assumed black people didn't like the sea much.

As excited as the kids were, they were also incredibly tired and after a short while we headed back to the enchanting apartment. After a very quick bath, before they fell asleep in the water, and donning pyjamas, it was then a question of where to put them. We certainly didn't want to use the sofa-bed because of the danger of early risers and inquisitive window activities. I contemplated putting all three kids in the double bed, with Ziggy and I having one of the single beds each, but he vetoed that idea very quickly. In the end Vicki and Leon shared one bed, top and tail fashion, as the beds were too narrow for them to sleep side by side even as small as they were, whilst lucky Brad had the other tiny bed all to himself.

Next morning, after a bowl of cereal, which we'd had the foresight to purchase from a nearby store the night before, and a cup of tea from the meagre provisions supplied in the apartment, we decided to check out the Malibou Hotel before taking the kids down to the beach. The hotel was very nice. Ziggy enquired if they had rooms available and was told that a family suite would only become available on the Monday, so he booked it immediately.

The kids had a whale of a time on the beach. We bought the obligatory buckets and spades and they played happily between dips in the warm Indian Ocean. We eventually decided it was time to get some food and after our previous experience decided we'd rather 'eat in' so we called at the supermarket we'd bought the breakfast cereal from and stocked up with sufficient provisions to last us as far as Monday breakfast.

We couldn't find any booze in the shop so Ziggy asked if sales were limited to Bottle Stores, like in Zambia. The shop assistant confirmed this was the case and kindly gave us directions to the nearest one, but as we were walking out the door she said, "But you won't get anything now. They closed at 1pm."

It was a quarter past.

"But they open again later, eh?" he asked hopefully.

"No," she laughed. "I'm afraid you've had it now until Monday morning."

As we slunk out into the street she called again.

"And just so that you know, restaurants with bars don't open on a Sunday either."

It was a religious thing apparently.

Our wonderful South African holiday was going pear-shaped before it had hardly begun.

The majority of what you have read here, dear reader, was recounted in a hand-written letter, as opposed to my normal type copy, to my parents back at their pub in England…

"….. so that is what has happened so far. I don't know if you have had trouble reading some of my ramblings, but if you have, you can blame it on the South African licensing laws. It's their fault that all I've had to drink tonight is duty-free whisky, and to be honest I'm feeling a bit squished.

As you can see this has turned into quite a long letter so I think I'd better post it before it needs sending parcel post. All I have to do in the morning is find the Post Office. If you're reading this then you'll know I succeeded.

Good night. xxxxxxxxx "

* * * * *

The following morning I left Ziggy trying to explain to his bosom pal Gloria that we were pulling out, and I went in search of the post office, which she assured me was close by. In my absence Ziggy was having considerable difficulty persuading her to give him a refund on the nights we were not going to be staying. It was his own fault, the silly man.

It was only when we checked into the Malibou Hotel, later that Monday morning, that we established they were only able to accommodate us for four nights. It hadn't occurred to us that the hotels would be full for Easter which, being the last major public holiday in South Africa before winter set in, was apparently always busy.

The hotel was a vast improvement on the apartment, even if it was short-lived, as was the lovely weather we'd been having. Tuesday and Wednesday it poured with rain all day, so we spent most of our time hopping between different shops, stocking up on all sorts of wondrous goodies. It wasn't much fun for the kids, although they were somewhat appeased when we diverted via the toy departments.

Ziggy had conceded that it was time we hired a car. Not for us the Avis or Hertz facility. He said if we went 'economy' it would leave us more money to spend on other things. He said George had recommended a car hire company which was quite 'reasonable', and phoned them.

After our experience of the 'excellent' apartments recommended by George, I was a little wary of his taste for car-hire but, of course, this was 'man decision' stuff so any objections I might have put forward were pointless.

He phoned the RAW Car Hire Agency and, as their offices were out of town, a man arranged to collect us and take us there. He pitched up in a huge but very dodgy looking emerald green Chevy which wasn't much of an advertisement for his car hire business.

He battled to get it into second gear.

"I've only just collected this one from the garage," he said by way of reassurance, "so I'm not familiar with it."

We drove, amidst crashing gears, for about 15 minutes, eventually arriving at his 'office'. He took Ziggy through the door of an old portacabin, which bore a flaking wooden sign confirming that this was the RAW Car Hire Agency. It seemed an appropriate name.

While the kids and I stood outside, gazing at the motley collection of cars in the yard, Ziggy handled the paperwork. After much haggling he arranged that we would return the car to the airport on the Monday and the car man would meet us there.

"So which out of this bunch of battered bangers is ours for the week?" I asked when he exited the office, gesturing towards what should have graced a scrap yard.

"He's given us this one," he replied, nodding towards the heap of junk we had arrived in.

"You've got to be kidding me!"

"Don't worry," said my nearest and dearest, "he said it's just had a new clutch fitted and that's why it's a little stiff."

I kept my mouth closed.

Days passed largely without incident. We visited a few places of interest and, as the hotel had an excellent babysitting service, actually managed to go out a couple of nights on our own.

On the first night we decided to treat ourselves to a special meal at a seafood restaurant on the harbour. I don't recall what Ziggy had but I ordered the crab salad.

Before we left England in 1980, Ziggy used to buy crabs' claws from the fishmonger at our local bi-weekly market in Burton. We would sit at our breakfast bar in the kitchen, with a pot of claws, two pairs of nutcrackers, a chilled bottle of crisp dry wine, and some toothpicks, and feast on the white crab meat. Much to Ziggy's distaste, I would sprinkle mine with malt vinegar. Considering how delicious they had been, when we lived so far from any coast, I couldn't wait to try crab fresh from the ocean.

I was quite surprised when the crab came in the form of rectangular sticks and coloured slightly pink on the outside, but figured this must be a special way of presenting it.

As I tucked into the first one I was quite surprised at the lack of crab flavour, but figured my taste-buds must have been compromised by the sip of wine I had just taken. I tried a second, accompanied by the salad, and when that didn't taste of much either, I supposed I must have put too much salad on my fork with it. I tried again, with the crab meat only. Nothing!

"Ziggy, have a taste of this. I can't find much crab flavour here, and the texture isn't very crab-like either."

He took half a stick on his fork and slowly ate it.

"I don't know what this is," said my husband, "but it certainly doesn't taste like any crab I've had before."

He called the waiter over.

"What is this?" Ziggy asked, pointing to the remaining sticks of stuff on my plate.

"Crab sticks, Sir," answered the waiter.

"But it doesn't taste like it has any crab in it."

"That's what they're called, Sir. By everyone."

"Well, perhaps everyone hasn't tasted real crab, which I find strange in a

48

coastal city," responded Ziggy.

Flicking his blonde hair from his eye, the waiter turned to me.

"Would you like me to take this away and bring you something else, Madam?" he enquired rather tartly.

"Yes, please. And no, thank you, I won't bother with anything else. I'll wait for dessert," I said.

My plate was whisked away. After Ziggy had finished his main course I completed my meal with a mediocre ice cream.

We didn't linger long after that, and in the absence of any obliging waiter walked to the reception desk to pay our bill. When it was presented to him Ziggy looked somewhat surprised.

"I see you've charged us for the crab. I'm not paying for something my wife couldn't eat."

"One moment," said the till operator brusquely, and disappeared smartly. He returned with the manager of the establishment.

"What's the problem?" asked surly manager.

"I'm not paying for this meal," said Ziggy, pointing to the crab salad specified on the bill, "it was not what my wife ordered."

"I can assure you Sir, that your wife was given the crab salad. And I understand that she managed to eat half of it before complaining."

"She ate as much as she did in order to try and find the crab. Which she couldn't. And neither could I, when I tried some of it."

"You foreigners are all the same," said the irate manager, "always trying to get a meal without paying for it. If you don't pay for it I shall call the police!"

"Call who the devil you like," retorted Ziggy "but you'll get no more money out of me."

At which he put down on the counter the exact amount of our bill, less the cost of the non-crab salad and we walked out.

One thing which took me completely by surprise as we drove along the seafront at the beginning of the week was the posting of huge notices. We simply hadn't looked close enough at the beach on that first Saturday morning to see the area was designated to *Whites Only*. Further along *Asians Only* proclaimed one board. *Blacks Only* stated another. And a third read *Coloureds Only*. I couldn't believe that there were designated bathing areas for whites, blacks and those 'in between'. That explained why I had only seen white faces on the beach across from the Malibou on that first day.

I had heard of South Africa being an Apartheid country of course, but to be honest had not given it much thought. 'Non-White' people had been an integral part of my life in England and now, living in a country with predominantly black people was similar, except that the colour ratio was reversed. But there, in Durban, the stark reality of enforced segregation was blatantly evident.

During the course of our stay we were to come across other facilities and service areas with similar notices, and a couple of bars with *Whites Only* emblazoned next to their open doors. This was so different to England and

Zambia where anyone could go wherever they wanted, and keep company with whomsoever they pleased.

Friday approached rapidly and we had to find somewhere else to stay for the last three nights. We made enquiries with the Malibou concierge. She mentioned a few possibilities.

"I think you might find this interesting," she said. "The Umhlanga Sands Hotel. It's very new. In fact I don't think they've quite finished building it yet."

She must have seen the look on my face.

"Oh, but it's perfectly alright. There are people already staying in it. I believe it is part hotel, part timeshare apartments, and they just haven't finished furnishing all of those yet."

"And," she went on, "Umhlanga Rocks is a lovely resort, about fifteen kilometres north of here. It really is very nice."

So we headed out early on the Friday morning lest we needed to find somewhere else to stay. We really hoped this wouldn't turn out to be another one of our now regular holiday screw-ups.

As we drove up to the place it did look quite impressive. Ziggy parked the green heap on the edge of the forecourt for a quick getaway, in case it turned out to be different to what we expected once we got inside. It certainly was.

It was fantastic.

As the receptionist explained all the facilities the hotel had for its guests, we couldn't believe our ears, or our eyes, once we had settled ourselves in.

We were given one of the timeshare apartments which turned out to be almost twice the size of the one we'd had at the Hoffman Seaboard, and it was beautifully furnished and well equipped. We dumped all our bags and hastened down to the ground to inspect all the facilities.

There was a huge landscaped area with tables and chairs and sunbeds laid out on the well-kept lawns which surrounded two swimming pools, the largest of the two having a paddling pool section for kiddies. There was a little outside playground, and inside a fully staffed crèche, or nursery, where the kids could be left to play safely with an amazing assortment of toys and games. There were three or four restaurants, a couple of shops and a hairdressing salon, a six-lane bowling alley and a disco which sometimes doubled as a cinema. And, of course a vast array of bar facilities.

Why the hell hadn't we come here for the entire holiday?!

We were so cross, yet so happy to have now found this place.

The crappy car from RAW never moved from the spot once Ziggy had parked it in the hotel's car park.

What a wonderful end to our holiday it was.

On the morning of our departure we left the hotel early as we needed to call at one of the large department stores in town before making our way to the airport.

On one of our shopping forays in a homeware shop called Game, I had spotted a hostess trolley on 'Special'. I showed it to Ziggy, reminding him that we had encountered these at friends' houses, and they had said what a bonus these compartmentalised heated trolleys were when catering for large meals.

"Get it," he said, and wandered off to do more 'man' shopping.

I searched out a store assistant.

"If I buy this, does it pack down, because we want to take it to Zambia?"

"Oh yes, Madam. We have more in stock, still in the original packaging. I will take your details at the sales counter," he went on, "and you will be able to collect it from our rear loading bay, at your convenience. I can tell them what day to expect collection if you don't want to take it now."

This was all very civilised and convenient, so I went through the appropriate formalities and my American Express card did very nicely, thank you.

So on the Monday morning we were waiting outside the loading bay of the Game store at start of business to collect our purchase.

What a surprise we got. The store assistant had obviously not fully understood my question when I had asked if it 'packed down'. Ziggy and I had both thought it would be dismantled and packed into a flat box, for reconstruction. We thought wrong. The box containing the hostess trolley was about the size of our two largest suitcases, put together!

We hadn't been worried about the excess weight of our purchase. We had bought a quantity of prepaid Unaccompanied Baggage Vouchers when we'd got our tickets specifically for this sort of situation. But the problem was how to fit it in the car with the rest of our luggage?

We needed to do an urgent rethink and a repack.

We tried to fit the trolley on the back seat with the kids, but couldn't even get it through the door. Eventually we managed to fit it more or less into the boot, but the only things which would fit in the boot with it were our pieces of hand baggage. Of course the boot didn't close. Ziggy had to go back into the shop, the front entrance being round the other side of the block, to buy some rope to tie down the boot and through the handles of the smaller bags to avoid them falling or being 'helped out' along the course of our journey. Then all we had to do was fit the five suitcases, two adults and three kids inside the car.

We managed to squeeze four cases in the back then the kids clambered in over the driver's seat, while I sat on the passenger seat with the remaining suitcase on my lap and my handbag around my neck like a horse-feed bag.

Then, with his knees almost up to his chest, (he'd had to push the front seats forward as far as possible) Ziggy attempted to drive the over-laden tin can to the airport. It was a good job we'd made an early start because as it spluttered and coughed, I don't think he managed to get the car beyond third gear during the entire journey.

The owner of the Rent A Wreck vehicle (yes, that was actually what RAW stood for) did not seem to appreciate our inventive use of his vehicle, as he watched us struggle to offload all our stuff onto two airport trolleys.

Perhaps we'll be blacklisted by RAW on any future visit to Durban, I thought. *How disappointing!*

Our check-in for the Johannesburg flight went very smoothly and we were able to have our suitcases and the hostess trolley checked right through to Lusaka. It's a pity the same couldn't be said for the passengers.

When we arrived in Johannesburg, and presented ourselves at the Zambia Airways desk, we were told we were 'wait-listed' as the flight to Lusaka was overbooked. We pointed to the 'confirmed' status on our tickets but this didn't hold any water with the dragon at the desk. We were told to check again at 11:45 to see if we'd be included on the flight. Thirty minutes later we were told that the flight had been delayed until 16:45. At five o'clock it was finally confirmed that we hadn't made the grade, but our luggage had, and was now winging its way to Lusaka without us.

The dragon said we should try to get a flight to Salisbury (now Harare) in Zimbabwe the next morning, from where we would take a further flight to Lusaka. Ziggy had been trying to do that for the past two hours (anticipating our lack of luck on the booked flight) but the woman at the Salisbury flight desk didn't want to take his booking until she knew that we were off the original flight, 'because it takes a long time to get flight confirmations'. She obviously had something else scheduled for her attention that afternoon.

Once it was confirmed that we were off the direct flight, our detour booking was accepted and confirmed. Whilst waiting for this process to be completed, Ziggy had booked us into the nearby Holiday Inn for the night.

As we left the desk we were wished a 'pleasant evening'. I won't repeat what Ziggy said, but it began with, "Why don't you …"

We exited the airport to find there was not a taxi to be seen.

"Look," said Ziggy pointing to the blazing lights of the Holiday Inn, "it's only just over there, we can walk that far."

We traipsed across the airport carpark until we reached a dual carriageway. Thankfully it wasn't too busy so we quickly crossed over to come up against one of those curvy, one-metre-high metal crash barriers. We lifted the kids and bags over, before scrambling over it ourselves to find that on the other side, clumps of overgrown grass had hidden the existence of a *donga*, a wide, deep storm-water ditch.

The fact that the sun had abandoned the sky half an hour or so earlier did not make for easy observation of hidden obstacles, nor navigation.

We stumbled down the bank into the ditch then walked along it until we found an area where it looked relatively easy to climb out on the other side. We pushed the kids up the bank in front of us, but had to return for Leon who lost his footing and rolled back down to the bottom. We were certainly grateful it hadn't rained for the past few days in Johannesburg.

We walked through more long grass and round some bushes, telling the kids to 'sing something' so that we knew they were still with us, until we came up against a six-feet high chain-link fence. With the hotel now only about 200 metres away on the other side of a car park, we walked beside the fence until we came to a broken section which had been prised back, giving access about a metre high.

As we crawled through, dragging our kids and bags behind us, we speculated that perhaps we had not been the first group of displaced passengers to trek this wild passage.

We got some very strange looks as we eventually staggered up to the reception desk of this international hotel, with no suitcases, no sign of a following taxi driver and, as the saying goes, looking like we'd been dragged through a hedge backwards. Little did they know that our adventure greatly surpassed that, as far as rough experiences went.

The kids were far too tired to want to eat, so went straight to bed. We weren't far behind them.

The following morning saw us back at the airport (taking a taxi this time) where we caught the flight to Salisbury, then moved quickly through for the next leg, to Lusaka.

We arrived in Zambia to be told by the girl behind the Zambia Airways desk in Lusaka, that there was only one flight up to the Copperbelt that afternoon.

"It already looks full. Would you like to be put on standby?" she asked.

After I'd climbed back down from the ceiling, I said, "Thanks, but no thanks."

Ziggy enquired about the following morning and was told by another clerk that he thought that one was full too, but he couldn't check because all the phones in the airport were 'down'. Ziggy had already established that fact when he tried to phone Rhinestone's offices to explain why he'd not pitched for work that morning.

He took a taxi, together with a couple of our suitcases, into town and managed to borrow one of the company cars to collect us and the rest of our *katundu* (Nyanja word for 'luggage') from the airport. After securely locking most of our belongings into an empty room at Rhinestone's Lusaka offices, we booked into the Intercontinental Hotel for the night, planning to drive up to Kitwe the next morning.

Ziggy arranged to borrow an estate car from Rhinestone for our trip northwards and had noticed that the company's British Leyland land-train (an extremely large truck) was also driving up to Kitwe on the same day, carrying a load of scrap steel. To make a little more room in the car for the kids, he arranged for our large, well-packed hostess trolley to be taken on that. As was customary, the vehicle was also taking a guard riding shotgun (unarmed), who would keep his eyes on the back of the truck whenever it came to a halt or a slow uphill stretch during its trip, to ensure nothing was 'lifted' by thieving hands.

I tried to imagine people stealing huge lengths of metal off the back of the truck, when it stopped at traffic lights, but failed miserably. However I was delighted with the arrangement for the safety of our trolley.

The car was filled up with petrol, oil and water, carried two spare wheels and two bottles of water (plus 5 suitcases, 2 bags, 3 kids, and 2 adults) and finally set off, giving instructions to the land train driver to stop should he see us on the roadside.

Twenty four kilometres outside Lusaka the car broke down.

So the kids, the luggage and I waited in the car for over an hour while Ziggy thumbed a lift back into Lusaka.

I was not happy about this situation. We were on a slight bend in the road, so could only see about fifty metres in either direction. There was a huge plantation of maize on one side of the road and the tall plants swayed and rustled in the breeze. On the other side were lots of bushes and long 'elephant grass'. This meant that we wouldn't see anyone approaching from any direction until they were virtually upon us. It would be fair to say I was pretty scared as we sat there.

I had of course locked all the doors, and the windows were opened only enough to provide us with fresh air to breath. But it was incredibly hot, even in this cooler month of April.

And there was nothing to do.

I Spy ran out very quickly, due to a lack of subject matter. We soon got bored with nursery rhymes and in my strained mental state I was in no frame of mind to make up fairy tales. Brad tried to entertain us with some Fozzie Bear (Muppets) jokes, but as these mostly involved movement and falling over, it restricted his repertoire. Anyway, we'd heard them all before and nobody but Brad found them very funny.

Then Leon gave it his very best shot. He sang us a story. The tune was rather nondescript but his story was rather inventive about a monkey going on holiday to Nanny and Grandad's pub in England. All was going well until the monkey was accidentally locked in the cellar where a big spider was hiding behind one of the beer barrels and Vicki got scared. Brad naturally jumped on this bandwagon and tickled the back of Vicki's neck sending her into a screaming frenzy. Oh, what fun we had.

As I was trying to break up the fight on the back seat, Ziggy arrived in the land train. This was followed closely by two mechanics in a *bakkie* (Afrikaans for a small open-backed van or pick-up). They rummaged around under the bonnet of our car and said if they towed it back to Lusaka they could get it fixed by the afternoon.

"Okay, but don't bother bringing it back here, we'll go up in this," Ziggy said, cocking his thumb towards the land train.

And so we all piled in. The passenger/guard was demoted to riding on the back of the truck, amidst the scrap metal, hostess trolley and our five suitcases. Then three kids and two adults, with two large pieces of cabin-baggage and a handbag, climbed into the cab alongside the driver. It was very 'cosy'.

It took us five hours, with a break, to travel the 360 kilometres to Kitwe in that 40-ton truck. It was quite an experience.

Thus, in grand style, ended our holiday of a lifetime.

7
Lotsa Dogs with Other Stuff

Dear Cathy,

I thought a quick note was in order to let you know what's happening. Things have returned pretty much to normal now, no theatre productions to worry about for some time, just a whole store-load of clothing to make for my private customers.

I'm also concentrating on making our meals a bit more interesting than they've been for a while. Aubergines are the veggie of the moment as we have a glut of them in our garden. And due to a hailstorm of mangos from our trees I also made some mango chutney last week. It is obviously my most successful batch so far, as Brad has been asking for it on bread for his breakfast, dinner and tea.

We have also been up to our eyeballs in dogs.

We noticed a few weeks ago that Sally was getting incredibly fat, and as we hadn't increased her food rations at all, it became clear that she was pregnant. The only trouble being we weren't sure who the father was – our young Irish Setter or her brother Foxwell. Unfortunately it has turned out to be her brother. Not good.

She had TEN puppies though three died within the first few hours. They have the run of the area under the car port and we have had to put boards all around to contain them. If they got out into the main garden they would be able to escape under the front gates. One pup in particular grabs my attention. I've called her Stumpy as another pup appears to have bitten off half her tail. She is very ambitious and manages to escape on a regular basis. She puts her feet on the top of the restraining board then claws her way up the board until she can fall down on the other side. I'm beginning to wonder if she's a crossbreed – dog and cat!

One by one the pups began to die. This saddened us greatly, but we had to be realistic. A litter from brother and sister is not a good thing, with possible health and temperament problems. Fortunately Peter had been so enchanted with Stumpy that he asked if he could have her. In case the other deaths were being caused by any infection, we let him take her at the earliest opportunity once she was weaned from Sally. We were delighted as we knew he would take good care of her. Thankfully she grew into a lovely dog and he never had any problems with her at all.

We immediately had Sally spayed to avoid a repeat situation. A few months down the line we had a different problem with Foxwell. Losing his partner's interest did not suppress his sex drive and he was frequently seen strolling around with a substantially exposed willy pointing in all directions, causing considerable curiosity amongst the children. The potential for a medium-sized dog humping someone's leg was bad enough, but given that the kids were less than the hip-height of an adult, it presented an even more unsavoury proposition.

I was explaining our dilemma to friends at the Club when a bachelor guy we knew said he had been thinking of getting a dog but didn't want the hassle of raising one from a puppy. We agreed that the coincidental timing was such that he was clearly meant to take over Foxwell. It was a win-win situation.

Shortly thereafter we had the opportunity to take on an Alsatian pup. She was a beautiful little thing who we named Cola, so we were devastated when she contracted that dreadful puppy virus, parvo, at twelve weeks old, from which she never recovered.

Many months later a friend of ours told us her dogs had mated and she had some beautiful Rhodesian ridgeback-cross pups up for grabs, would we like one? Is the Pope a Catholic? They were absolutely gorgeous. We chose the biggest from the litter and collected him when he was six weeks old. Then came the naming challenge.

When we first moved to Zambia and found, to my delight, that it was essential to have dogs, we took on an old Irish setter bitch from someone who was leaving the country. Her name was Brandy (the dog, not the woman who left the country). We also bought our first puppy.

Ziggy's boss, Doug, and his wife, Molly, had a highly pedigreed Irish setter and, just after we arrived in Zambia, he had sired a litter of puppies. Molly convinced us that we should buy one of them to keep Brandy company. He came with a fancy pedigree name which we had no intention of using so needed to give him a family name. We figured it had to be something which went with Brandy. After much deliberation we settled on Coke. Original, or what?

Sally and Foxwell were already used to their non-drink names though where the devil our friends got the name Foxwell from I have no idea! But we vowed that any dogs we might get in future would be named after drinks.

We tossed around several ideas for our new pup, which we knew would grow into quite a big dog and eventually came up with 'Bass'. Bass was the name of one of the major breweries in our home town. It was the company I used to work for before the kids came along, as well as the brewery which owned my parents' pub. The famous Bass Pale Ale was also about the same colour as our new pup.

Bass grew into a beautiful, huge specimen of a dog, looking distinctly ridgeback. A few years later the kids and I would take him for walks and were highly amused when, because of his size and colour, the locals would point and utter 'hey simba' (lion) whilst quickly crossing the street to get as far away from him as possible.

It was quite appropriate that he be compared to a big cat as he was an absolute pussy cat. He didn't have an aggressive bone in his body, although I must admit that his skills as a protector never had to be put to the test.

When I had written my letter to Cathy, Ziggy asked me to tell her that he had planned to write a letter to her husband, his pal Pete, but he couldn't because his hand was all bandaged up.

I felt the need to enlarge on his comment.

"Now don't get all sympathetic. The cause of the break was because he took a swipe at Leon for some reason a couple of weeks ago but missed and hit a door jamb instead. He walked around in agony for ten days before getting it x-rayed to find he'd broken a bone in his hand. Serves the fool right, I say.

Although I have no room to talk myself.

A couple of days after Ziggy's incident, Brad and Leon had sneaked their breakfast to eat in Leon's bedroom for some reason. I knew nothing about this until I heard a crash. I rushed down the corridor to find Brad had broken one of my best plates so I picked up the broken pieces, gave Brad a hiding, took Leon's plate off him, then stormed back to the kitchen. As I marched in I skidded on milk they'd spilt and went arse over tit, finishing up with bruised bones and skinned knees.

These bloody kids must have guardian angels of note."

* * * * *

If you have read *Into Africa*, you may recall the saga of Ziggy's driving test. If not I can tell you that he had to take it three times before he passed. When we were well into our second Rhinestone contract I decided that it was about time I took mine, so I made a booking.

When the day arrived, I had to take the test in a company *bakkie* because Ziggy's car was off the road and the only replacement car available was slightly defective. Neither the headlights nor the speedo worked, and we thought the driving test examiner might notice the latter.

Very early on the morning of my test, Peter was dashing all over the place trying to find a roadworthy *bakkie* for me to use, then I had to take it out for half an hour to get used to it and practice 'proper' driving before my test at 11 o'clock. What a performance! For the Zambian test you had to use hand signals all the time. My arm was paddling around like a windmill in a gale.

Ziggy had already taken me around the test route, which was always the same, on the previous Sunday morning.

A regular sight in Kitwe was the 'learner truck', a 4-ton, drop-side vehicle sporting well-worn L-plates, which could have as many as a dozen enthusiastic 'supporters' standing in the back, as some optimistic soul took truck-driving lessons around the test route. You could always tell if the driver was actually taking his test as there would be only two passengers in the cab (as opposed to the customary four) and no more than three devotees in the back. I often wondered if, when the driver eventually passed his test, he would be capable of driving along any other roads.

Now Peter took me along to some waste ground where I practiced reversing between two rows of barrels, and turning in from both the left and right sides. I only hit them the first time and after that it was a doddle.

It was a known fact that virtually nobody in Kitwe passes his driving test on the first attempt, especially not a *Mzungu* madam (white woman). But maybe it depended on who you took with you. My friend Big Lynda, who ran the Club office, offered to go with me. And she happened to be friends with the examiner.

Of course, I am not saying that her presence had any bearing on the issue. Oh, no. I am sure my driving was simply impeccable, because I passed. First time.

Nice lady, Lynda.

* * * * *

But friends in the right places wasn't all Lynda was good for. Lynda, Gill Lonsdale and I, with help from a couple of other ladies, had somehow managed to get ourselves involved in catering.

The first major event was catering for a special cabaret, which was to take place in what would become the 'intimate surroundings' of the main bar at the Little Theatre.

It was quite an ambitious production, with a live band to accompany the various singers and dance routines. A suitable area was given over as a temporary stage which was surrounded by tables and chairs accommodating the guests.

As we slaved away in the kitchen, the three-course meal was served by members temporarily acting as waiters. At least we did get to see most of the show, which began after the main course had been served. It was a huge success.

Some months later, Peter Heath and Karen Robinson produced a cabaret along similar lines, but on the stage in the auditorium. This was so successful that the theatre committee decided that a similar theme should be adopted for this year's NKAS Annual Awards Ball.

I wrote about it to my folks back in the UK.

Dear All,

So sorry for the long delay in writing but, as usual, things have been quite hectic here.

Last Saturday we had the annual Awards Ball and for the week leading up to it I was up to my eyes in breadcrumbs and chopped onions and herbs, making stuffing balls for 120 people.

It was organised by Big Lynda (from the office), Gill Lonsdale and myself, and helped by Dianne, Sheila, Joan Brandrick and a few others doing flowers.

A dozen tables, all of which seated ten diners, were positioned on the main stage. Each was adorned with white table cloth with red overlay and napkins, and featured a floral centrepiece and complimentary tub of cigarettes.

The menu consisted of an egg mayonnaise starter followed by soup, then the main course of roasts, beef and pork, fresh vegetables, stuffing balls, apple sauce and gravy. Dessert offered a choice of profiteroles or trifle and concluded with coffee and After Eight mints. Imported wine and liqueurs were on sale.

The day in question was one of wonderfully organised chaos. We had Peter running around fetching ice and bits and pieces from helpers' houses. Benton was there from 4:15 to help with the ongoing washing up, being joined later by a few other house-servants to assist with collection and washing of the evening's dishes.

Having grabbed a few bites to eat along the way, I finished my stint in the kitchen and eventually took my seat at our table on the stage to enjoy the rest of the evening.

We were entertained by a short cabaret which was accompanied by a hired band. As the stage was pretty full already with the tables and cabaret artists, a temporary stage, propped up on stilts and beer crates, had been erected over the front auditorium seats for the band.

After the cabaret, came the Awards ceremony.

All award winners were given a bottle of champagne with which to celebrate. I'm trying to think if there were any award winners you would know – not many I'm afraid.

Best Actress: won by my friend Janet McDermott.

Critics Award: which is given to someone who had been rated highly but who hadn't received a specific award for either acting or production - Blacky Hall won that.

Best Costumes: Guess who? Yes, yours truly, thank you, thank you, thank you! That was for the costumes for Mary Stuart.

Then there was another award which is given out by the Theatre Council, called the Hughes Award. It is given to a person or persons who have generally done a lot for the theatre in many different ways. You could have knocked us down with a feather when we heard them call,

"And this Award goes to Ann and Ziggy Patras."

Bloody hell, talk about amazed! As you would expect, Ziggy had to be virtually dragged up to collect the Award and bottle of champers.

I must say I feel highly honoured that we should win this, particularly when I could name at least a dozen other people who I think have done at least as much as we have for the club.

Needless to say, we celebrated appropriately.

It was about midnight when the band started up for dancing, then after an hour we had a disco for a while before reverting back to the band again. We left at 1:30 although several of our pals stayed on until 4:00. We were told there were still others hanging around after that, but they were too pissed to know what time they eventually went home.

Everyone agreed that this was the best Awards Ball ever put on. I must admit, for me it would take some beating!

8
The Auction

As Ziggy's work at the Cobalt Plant was nearing completion, the question was being raised of what he would do next.

We had heard that life in Botswana was much easier than Zambia as sharing a border with South Africa, basic food items, as well as luxuries, would not be such a problem to acquire. Rhinestone's holding Group had a company in Botswana with a position which might become available and Ziggy was asked if he'd be interested in taking it up. We decided that Ziggy should pursue this move.

Unfortunately the availability of the post was dependent on the engineer already working there. Apparently he wasn't sure whether he was going to stay in Botswana, to work on the new project, or move to work on one which was coming up in Tanzania. Until that was clarified, nothing could be confirmed for Ziggy, although Rhinestone were sure they would have work for him somewhere to warrant the offer of a second two-year contract for us. We would simply have to sit it out and see. We were quite happy with this arrangement.

Occasionally the expatriate community would hold an auction. When people reached the end of their contract and decided not to renew, they invariably had quite a few possessions that other Kitwe residents, be they expats or locals, would give their eye teeth for. Many of these were cheap, simple items, but unavailable in Zambia.

Kitwe Auctioneers would be called in to conduct this auspicious event. Sometimes the departing expats would not have enough goodies to stimulate a good turnout, so friends and acquaintances were encouraged to join in if they had any unwanted items to sell. The prices paid for some things could be ludicrously high and a fast buck or two could be made if you were the seller.

At the end of May, John, an acquaintance from the theatre club, and his wife, were leaving Zambia and had space in their auction for a few more goodies. With our potential move to Botswana at the back of my mind, I delved into my crammed cupboards to see if there was anything I didn't need which could be sold instead of carting them to a new location. There were quite a few items.

The auctioneer needed to know whose items he was selling so I made a list and passed it to John. On the Saturday morning of the auction I arrived with my bits and pieces and displayed them in appropriate places.

From 11:00 until 13:45 in the afternoon, people filtered in and out of the property, checking out the various items for sale. The auctioneer had a 'guard' placed in each room to ensure none of the goods disappeared before the sale began. All kitchen stuff, and other small goods, were placed on trestle tables in the garden to make them more visible to the potential buyers.

Then the mini-crowd was kept at bay while everything was returned to a neat and tidy order before the auctioneer began his spiel.

"Ladies and Gentlemen, welcome here today. We have a wonderful selection of items for you to buy and we implore you to spend as much as you like. All items on display are for sale, except for the trestle tables and items specifically marked 'Not for Sale' such as the kitchen sink and Mavis, my assistant, here."

Appropriate laughter wafted around the garden.

"All items are sold for cash only, no lay-bys, hire-purchase or 'pay you on Friday' will be considered. All electrical goods have been tested to make sure they work so it's no good bringing something back tomorrow saying it doesn't. And if you bought something that doesn't do what you thought it would, chances are you bought a colander instead of a mixing bowl. In simple terms all items are sold *as is* or, as the Afrikaners would say, *voetstoots*."

"Once your bid has been accepted and the money handed over, your purchase is your responsibility for safe keeping. All larger items may remain in-situ until the end of the auction but *all* items must be removed from these premises before 6pm, unless by prior arrangement with myself."

"Right!"

The loud crash of his gavel hit the mobile lectern, and the front row of bidders swayed back as one.

"Let's get this show on the road."

"First we have this magnificent plastic washing-up bowl complete with three cloths and a scrubbing brush. Am I bid three *kwacha?*"

And so it began.

The official exchange rate at the time was approximately K2, which was equal to £1 ($1.50). The prices people were prepared to pay for items not available in Zambia bore no resemblance to their original cost.

I managed to sell some early-years children's books, jigsaws and cot blankets (for the life of me, I cannot figure out why I should have brought cot blankets to Zambia). I also sold Pyrex dishes and duvet covers; a Bex Bissell carpet sweeper, and a cooker child-safety guard. A small non-stick saucepan, which you could pick up for about £1.50 in the Co-op, sold for K9; a stainless steel bread bin in good, but not perfect, condition sold for K21; and a portable radio, for which we paid £35, rocketed up to K150, about £75 in real money. I even got the equivalent of six quid for 11 disposable nappies (diapers) and half a box of nappy liners, which I would have bought from Boots in Burton for a couple of pounds.

In total I made K483.00, about £240 (US$350), an amazing figure for such paltry items.

I might have made slightly more were it not for one rather large lady, with customary baby strapped to her back. She hitched up her left buttock to rest on the edge of a trestle table. which tipped up, resulting in my stack of

Pyrex dishes sliding to the floor, breaking the largest one.

I think that must have preceded my downfall too.

Previously unnoticed by me, rugs of various sizes had been draped over bushes or fences to avoid being trampled upon. These were now removed for auction, one by one, and spread on the lawn to fully display their size and quality. I ended up buying the largest, which I figured would fit nicely in our lounge and help warm the room slightly during the colder months, together with a small one for our bedroom.

The logic of this move later baffled my husband somewhat when I admitted that not 20 minutes earlier, I had sold our carpet sweeper. These things happen.

But the folly of this action had not escaped my attention either, and should have then steered me towards the gate and an early departure from the remaining proceedings. Unfortunately curiosity got the better of me.

John, the guy whose house contents were being sold, had a rather superb model railway setup. I had always been fascinated by these and as a child I had found them, along with Meccano, far more interesting than dolls. John's arrangement was extensive, fully landscaped, with hills hiding tunnels; there were level-crossings and bridges; sidings and turntables; fields and hedges; a small village with a church and, of course, the obligatory station.

It was an L-shaped affair, set up in his spare bedroom, and was incredibly impressive. For all the stuff he had there I reckoned you'd have easily paid £600 (US$875) in the UK, but to an enthusiast in Zambia it must have been worth fifteen hundred *kwacha*.

Anyway, I happened to poke my head round the door when it was being auctioned. The bidding went K20 - K30 – K50 - K80 – K110 – K150 – K190 – K230 – K270 – K300 …

"Going for K300 once, going for K300 twice," the auctioneer was dragging it out very slowly, obviously hoping to raise it more than that, "going for K300 for the third ti…"

"K320!" came a shout.

Everyone turned round to look where this bid came from.

It was me!

"We have an offer of K320. Any advance on K320? This is the final offer of K320. Going for K320. Gone!"

I nearly passed out! What the blazes was I going to do with K320's worth of scenic model railway which, incidentally, was fixed solidly to the wall of a bedroom?

I disappeared off to the toilet and sat there calling myself all the stupid names under the sun for blowing almost two thirds of the proceeds of *my* sale on some blasted trains.

I thought, *Ziggy 'll kill me when I tell him about this.*

In jest, before leaving home, I had mentioned to him that John was selling his train set and that he didn't think many people were interested in it, and Ziggy had replied, also in jest, well buy it yourself. But the key word here is *jest*.

Still seated on the toilet I tried to justify my actions.

Well, it is fully automated and *there are still an awful lot of parts which haven't even been put on yet* and *it's far cheaper than buying the bits new.*

Try as I might, I didn't do a very good job of convincing myself, but hoped it would sound better when I put my case to Ziggy.

Eventually I plucked up the courage to go home and break the news to my dear husband. He took it very well, all things considered. In fact I actually thought he seemed quietly pleased without admitting to it.

But the train set trauma wasn't over yet. John had agreed that I could leave it there until I could get suitable transport to cart it off. On the Monday, which happened to be a public holiday, we had to get hold of not only a *bakkie* but also a carpenter and try to extricate it from John's bedroom wall. Even then it had to be cut into two pieces in order to get it out of the door. Once at home it would all have to be crated up ready to be taken down to Botswana. What a twit I was!

Of course, we didn't dare tell the kids about its existence. We hid the main frame in the garden shed, which we knew they never went into because that was where the gardener stored his work boots that gave off a rather obnoxious odour.

After all, we didn't want *them* playing with it. Train sets are not for kids!

9
A Trip Back and a Bottle of Milk

The end of our first two-year contract was upon us and although we still weren't sure what Ziggy would be doing when he renewed it, we had decided to take a six week holiday in the UK. Our holiday promised to be quite hectic.

We knew the first week would be filled catching up with everyone and the kids being spoilt rotten by their grandparents, aunts and uncles, not to mention the customers at my parents' pub in Burton upon Trent.

We wanted to drive down to the south-west of England where some of our Zambia friends had returned to live, as well as catch up with a couple of friends in Devon, then take a ferry over to the Channel Island of Jersey.

During another week of our leave we were able to hand the kids over to Ziggy's sister, Jady, who was going to take them, singlehanded, to Butlins Holiday Camp in Wales for a week of fun. I admired her courage.

But one of the most important issues by which the timing of these events was governed, was Brad's visit to the Ear, Nose, Throat (ENT) Specialist, to get his ears checked out again. We were pretty sure he would need surgery again to insert grommets, which proved to be the case.

The nice quiet week we anticipated spending without the kids went out the window when we discovered the state of our English property. For the past 18 months, we had placed the rental of our home in the hands of a respectable firm of estate agents who were supposed to ensure the rent was collected and the property looked after. The latest tenants having recently vacated, we went to check it out and were horrified to find that, amongst other things, it was in serious need of repair and redecoration.

It was an old house and we had done a lot of work on it. A large bedroom had been converted into a bathroom. We figured the recent tenants had never opened a window during their stay, because the walls were covered in mould. Such was the state of this bathroom that we spent our leisure week stripping the wallpaper, then scrubbing and treating the mouldy walls with fungicide, before eventually re-papering. The regular inspections which were part of the rental contract had obviously not been made.

Not wishing to repeat this procedure every time we came over on leave, we decided to sell our first home. The estate agents were initially delighted when we advised them of this, saying they would sell it in no time at all.

"I doubt you will," I said.

"Oh, I'm sure, Mrs Patras, we will soon find a buyer."

"Then you'll be able to send them straight to Raybould and Sons, who are now the estate agents who'll be selling it for us," I announced, "because after the useless job you made of looking after our property, you sure as hell aren't getting any more commission out of us!"

Most of the rest of our holiday was spent, as you might expect, shopping. Apart from clothes, food items and sewing supplies, we had decided to go wild on setting ourselves up with home entertainment items.

One of the customers at my parents' pub was an electrical retailer, with a store on the other side of the block of the pub. Barry said that if we bought all our requirements from him, rather than one of the large national stores, he would give us a substantial discount. We bought a new hi-fi system to replace the mediocre one we had purchased when our original equipment was stolen in 1981. We also bought a portable video player/recorder, and a video camera. The camera was large and weighty and had to be attached to the recorder unit by a long cable, though it was all very 'new age' at the time.

We purchased 20 three-hour blank VHS video tapes and, as he also owned a video rental company, and knowing that we were taking everything (in his words) 'to some godforsaken place beyond the equator', Barry kindly offered to record films onto the tapes for us.

At least, he said, we'd have something to watch before filling them up with shots of (hopefully not rampaging) elephants, lions, etc; kids' school concert performances and other things equally riveting. He said we could choose which videos we wanted, but having been off the main circuit, as it were, for the past two years, we had no idea what was available, so left the choice mostly to him, apart from a few kiddies' films we knew about.

Of course we then needed a television on which to watch all the videos he was going to record. We also splashed out on a microwave oven.

Extremely excessive import duty was charged on new electrical items entering Zambia. When we bought our air tickets we had also purchased some 'Unaccompanied Baggage' vouchers, knowing that we were going to be making some purchases in the UK. This meant the freight charges for all our packaged goodies could be paid for in *kwacha*. We checked in the boxes along with our luggage, though the boxes would then be placed on a cargo flight to Zambia.

Before we had left Lusaka international airport, on our flight to the UK, Ziggy had approached a customs official, saying that we were taking some goods out with us, some for repair, others simply for safekeeping, and that he required some specific paperwork so they would be allowed back in the country without paying duty on our return.

The official asked to see these goods but, sharp as a pin, Ziggy explained that, along with our luggage, they were already 'in the system' having been directed right through from Kitwe to London.

The official happily signed and stamped the paper, after having put a squiggly Z in the lower section of the form to ensure that no more items could be added to it.

Six weeks later, as we stood in the passageway of the Burton Arms, with all our sturdily packed boxes of goodies, Ziggy included details of our purchases on the customs form, on the lines which he had accidentally left blank between the amplifier and sewing machine which was purportedly in for repair.

Then it was time to leave. My folks, of course, were not pleased we were returning to Zambia for another two year contract, but having seen and heard how much we were enjoying our lives, they could fully understand it.

After I have been away on holiday, I'm always glad to be home. It had been wonderful to catch up with friends and family, and the shopping experiences were an absolute delight. But home now was Africa.

We were very warmly greeted by Peter and Benton and his family, as well as Rafael our dedicated night-guard and Clement the gardener. We bought all of them, including Benton's wife Christina and their kids, gifts of T-shirts, with which they were all absolutely delighted. There were also some extra treats for Peter and Benton, who had done such a grand job of looking after our home and dogs while we were away.

As I wandered around our house the only things missing were hand-prints and gecko droppings on the walls. Benton had been spring cleaning. I was sure my three little darlings would take no time at all in messing it all up again.

When all our new stuff arrived in Kitwe a few weeks later, Ziggy went along to collect it from the customs warehouse and paid the required duty. All thirty-five *kwacha* of it.

* * * * *

It was time to find out what was in store for Ziggy on the work front. It transpired that the engineer working in Botswana had decided to stay there for the new project.

Rhinestone had, as part of the company group, a manufacturing division in Kitwe which had slowly been going into decline. As there was little competition in this field, this should not have been the case and could only be put down to mismanagement. On his return Ziggy was asked if he'd be interested in running it, to try to get it back on an even keel.

It sounded like exactly the challenge he needed. Initially moving in as Engineer in Charge, within several months he was the official General Manager of a profitable little company.

* * * * *

A fresh introduction into our lives at the start of our new contract was the milk run. Those who were lucky enough, were invited to join one.

This is where a bunch of expats got together and arranged to buy milk direct from a farm. The groups usually consisted of about five families. Each family would take a turn each week to go to the farm to collect the milk. This involved having a load of bottles delivered to your house, which you would then take to the farm to be filled with fresh milk before returning them all to their rightful owners.

Those of you old enough might remember the small, one pint milk bottles which used to be delivered daily to homes in England. Well, our milk bottles were nothing like that!

Ours were ex-Coca Cola concentrate bottles with wide, metal screw-on tops and each bottle held five litres (or eight pints). The norm was for each family to be restricted to three bottles, but even that was a substantial haul when you had to fit fifteen of them into the boot of your car.

The key to this fascinating ritual was getting yourself invited onto a milk run in the first place. They were quite limited and highly sought after, requiring an expat family to leave Kitwe before a 'place' became available. If you were lucky their bottles were handed down too. If not, you had the unenviable task of trying to get the Coca Cola factory to sell you some.

You had to make sure that you didn't plan any weekends away from home when it was your turn to do the run or, if it was unavoidable, you had better make a plan for someone else to do your trip for you.

This might sound like a bit of a pain in the butt, just to get some milk, especially as milk was usually available in town. But this milk was so delicious that, if you were a milk lover, once you had tasted this fresh creaminess, anything else seemed like water.

Most people would leave the milk to stand in the bottles, in their fridges, for 24 hours before carefully syphoning off the cream, a thick, golden, three-inch layer which rose to the top of the bottle. This you would containerise and then use to enhance your puddings or cakes, with thickly poured cream, or whip it up for piped decoration. During a butter shortage, you could always whip it a little longer to provide homemade butter. The only thing I didn't try making was cheese.

All you had to do was make sure you handed your empty bottles to the family of the week before a prescribed time on whichever day your milk run took place, Saturday or Sunday; and have someone available to receive it when it was delivered back to your home a few hours later.

We were very lucky in that most of the time we had Peter working for us over the weekends, so he would take it in. And of course, when it was our turn for the milk run, quite often Peter would do it for us.

* * * * *

Talking of liquids has reminded me to enlarge upon a more popular drink.

Beer was quite a strong feature in Zambia and quite an anomaly in itself.

I had lived in Zambia for many months before I knew that the home grown beer had a name, *Mosi*. This was because there were never any labels on the bottles. But considering that it was the only beer available in the country at the time, there was really no need for a label. And it was a lager rather than the 'true' beer so familiar to us Brits in those days. Especially Brits like Ziggy and I who came from Burton upon Trent, which is just about the most famous brewery town in England.

There were two breweries in Zambia both owned by the aptly named Zambia Breweries (ZB). One was on the Copperbelt in Ndola, the other in

Lusaka. You would never guess they were brewing the same stuff because they tasted completely different. Thankfully Ndola made the better one.

The one which came from Lusaka, and which we were subjected to occasionally when the Ndola brewery broke down, was nauseating to the point that I wouldn't drink it.

When I was a kid I had a pony. Yes, yes, I know. I was talking about beer, but stay with me. I had a pony called Richard. Yes, that really was his name, and he lived in a field near the river Trent. This was about a half a mile away from the shop where I lived, which occupied a corner on the end of a row of terraced houses.

The long, narrow area that would normally have been a garden for our type of property, was concreted and given over to the storage of certain commodities for the shop. My grandmother's attempt at gardening, therefore, comprised pot plants in and around a small conservatory leading onto that area. And she liked to grow tomatoes.

Why you would grow tomatoes when you owned the best grocery/green grocery shop in the area I do not know. But growing tomatoes was Doris's one little love. That and cactus plants. She would grow two or three large pots of tomato plants each summer.

I was encouraged to ride Richard to the shop on a fairly regular basis on the chance that he could deliver to Doris a nice load of manure. She would put this in a bucket, add water to the brim, then after a couple of days of a stirring around, she would use the liquid to water her precious tomato plants (though not the cacti).

Lusaka-brewed beer reminded me of that slop. Not that I tried drinking the slop, you understand. But as you might imagine, this bucket full of horse manure gave off quite a distinct aroma, and the taste of the beer was like the smell of that slop. I wondered if the odd flavour to Lusaka beer was anything to do with the water supply, because the reason Burton was such a successful brewery town was something to do with the local water.

I can understand if you are now completely put off ever visiting Zambia in case you are forced to drink a Lusaka *Mosi*, but do not fear. After a few years, someone who knew what he was doing got involved at Lusaka and solved the problem so that their produce became more palatable.

There was, however, another issue involved with *Mosi* in those days. It was a culture problem, and I'm not talking about the African culture as in colourful *chitenge* cloth which Zambian women wore, or the African drums one could sometimes hear in the night. The culture I'm talking about is more biological.

You see, people would have many crates of empty bottles tucked away on their property. For weeks or even months, beer supplies could be restricted to two or three crates per person, so the majority of one's empties would sit unused, and often in the full sun in the backyard of a house. Then hey presto, ZB would be up and running at full tilt and folk would stock up as much as possible before the next shortage hit the scene.

So those beer crates which had been sitting in the sun for months were taken back into the brewery. They would, of course, go through the appropriate washing process before being once more filled and despatched. Unfortunately whatever cleansing process the brewery adopted wasn't always sufficient to remove all the gunk which had settled and dried in the bottom of the bottles. Strangely enough *Mosi* had no such inadequacies.

Whatever sturdy substance remained glued to the inside of the bottles, having been soaked in *Mosi* and shaken around in a crate for many days or possibly weeks, became dislodged and floated around inside like a semi-comatose goldfish. Cultures, which many scientists would be proud of, grew in those old brown bottles.

Many people preferred drinking their beer direct from the bottle, being already chilled and therefore able to maintain a cool temperature longer than a beer glass in the African heat. Apart from that, glasses were not exactly abundant in some places, having been broken, or more often stolen, until stocks were all but depleted.

Drinkers would first hold their bottle up to the light, to check for 'floaters', before taking their first sip of beer. If the barman of the drinking establishment was worth his salt, he would have checked the bottle's contents before removing the top, but not all remembered to do this, especially during busy periods.

I recall one afternoon at the Club, someone found what looked like a section of a toothbrush floating around in his beer. *Urgh!* Goodness knows how that got in there. I also heard that a couple of years earlier, a friend of a friend found a section of a mouse's tail in his beer.

During my beer-drinking days in Zambia, I came across many a bottle containing dubious floating substances, which were, of course, instantly disposed of down the nearest drain.

One day Ziggy and I were in a club we rarely visited. We were both drinking *Mosi* and I was lucky enough to be given a glass, a rare accessory in this particular establishment. Alas, it was a small glass, and accommodated only half the contents of the bottle. I had drunk the first half and poured the remainder into the glass, together with a glob of substance which resembled a combination of egg white and rotten mushroom.

Oh, for goodness sakes, I'm almost gagging here as I recall the incident.

I rushed off to the Ladies and hurled my insides down the toilet.

It was many, many months before I could face another *Mosi*, and I never, ever drank one before closely scrutinising the entire contents of the bottle.

10
Entertainment at its Best

One of the things not contained in any of the thirteen crates we initially shipped to Zambia was a television set. Ziggy and I had never really been big TV fans before we had the kids. We only bought one in England after we started our family and were forced to stay at home of an evening. Even then we were quite selective about what we watched.

As a result we never considered taking one to Zambia. Not only did we not know if a UK television would work over there, we didn't even know if they had television.

We soon found that they did, but it left a lot to be desired. Nevertheless there were a few classic programmes which we loved to watch. One in particular was a cookery programme which was aired once a week and bore no resemblance to the quality of the presentations we had been used to watching in England.

Once we left the temporary accommodation we were given on our arrival, the luxury of a television was no longer available to us. Only after buying the television during our recent visit to the UK, were we once again able to tune into the Zambian Broadcasting Service's sole channel.

We were delighted to find that the cookery programme was still being presented and, ensuring we avoided all social engagements on that particular evening, were comfortably seated in front of the screen when it began.

The presenter of the show, Elizabeth, would begin by telling us what she was going to make, then she would produce the various ingredients from under her counter, or from a table which was positioned behind her.

On the occasion I am going to describe to you, she told us she was going to make a *Frut Malingwe Tat* (Tart).

"First we will make the pastry," she explained, as she removed a large bowl from under the table, placing it on the counter.

"We will add to the bowl four handfuls of flour." (It would appear neither scales nor a cup were readily available.)

She reached for a small, yellow plastic bucket which had been set on the table and delved into it. She brought out the handfuls of flour which she tossed into her mixing bowl, from which a hazy white cloud arose before settling back down to coat the counter in a thin white film.

"Next we will add the butter."

She carefully peeled the paper from a half-pound slab of butter then looked around for her knife which was hiding in front of the mixing bowl. Once found, she glanced around further until she realised that her chopping board was on the table behind her. With knife and butter in hand she turned to the table behind her and continued,

"We need to ut … bu….er ..to ….all pie….s … ake it eas… to …nd " turning back to the camera, "into the flour. "

(The microphone suspended over her work station clearly was not geared to picking up speech when she worked on the rear table.)

She finished with a smile, throwing the roughly cut cubes of butter into the bowl, creating another minor flour fallout.

By this time Ziggy and I were sliding off our chairs as we tried to control our laughter lest we should miss any of this riveting viewing.

"Now," she said, "we rub the butter into the flour until it is small."

She began manipulating the contents of the bowl. This was a sturdy ceramic bowl, and from the angle the camera was positioned, you could not actually see what she was doing inside the bowl.

After about a minute of mysterious movement which more resembled a hand-washing ceremony, she imparted, "We must add water to this."

From a pink plastic jug she tipped an unknown quantity of water into the bowl and continued with her unseen procedure. Then she upended the bowl and a crumbling lump of whiteness, surrounded by a large quantity of semi-congealed particles, tumbled onto the counter.

Elizabeth swept all the errant crumbs up to the centre and tried to make them stick to the body of pastry, which seemed a little reluctant to adhere. I think she realised that she hadn't used sufficient water so she poured more from the pink jug onto the mass. That made quite a difference, and she proceeded to knead the ball of pastry until it had incorporated all the errant crumbs stuck to the table.

Her hands were now covered in globs of white gunge, reminding me of when we used to make flour paste glue for *papier maché* when I was a kid. Using a towel, she did manage to remove most of it from her fingers before moving on to the next stage of this demonstration.

With a good handful of flour sprinkled over the pastry ball, table and rolling pin (and probably the floor too) she rolled out the pastry to the desired size. This was not an easy task as sections of the dough, where the butter hadn't been incorporated quite as thoroughly as it should have been, stuck to the table as she tried to turn it. She eventually placed this over a shallow pie dish.

"Now we make the pastry fit the pie dish."

That went relatively smoothly as she eased the dough into the shape of the receptacle, only requiring a couple of pastry patches in the centre where it had split. I must say I was very impressed with the way she expertly held the dish aloft as she trimmed off the excess pastry from the rim.

"You must now cook the pastry in the oven but I won't cook this one because there isn't time. But I made one earlier. I shall fetch it," and she wandered off camera for what seemed like an age before returning with a perfectly baked pastry case.

However, she had some advice before continuing with the next stage in this fascinating demonstration.

"I just remembered, I should have put salt in the pastry, so make sure you add some when you make yours."

Given the precision with which she measured out her flour, we dreaded to think what quantity of salt her viewing public might add to their ingredients. (We were never informed of the quantity of butter to use.) Of course, it didn't end there.

"Now I shall make the filling."

She reached under the counter for another bowl, and then to an area off camera on her left for a small blue bucket.

"We shall use two handfuls of sugar," which she threw into the bowl, "and the rest of the butter.'

She turned to pick up the butter which had been hiding on the rear table.

Ah, so she hadn't used it all in the pastry!

For a short spell she beat the butter and sugar together with a large wooden spoon. Putting the bowl slightly to one side she then produced two large lemons and a grater. Holding the grater over the bowl she vigorously rubbed the lemon over the grater. Obviously this was not an easy operation because not all the lemon rind entered the bowl as the grater jerked around above it.

Placing the grater on the table she turned to the rear counter with her lemons and talked to herself before turning back with the two fruits cut in half. Using two hands she squoze (no such word, I'm told) squeezed the juice of each one into the bowl of sugar/butter, complete with several pips, or seeds. To her credit she did fish out some of the pips, though I fear not all of them.

"Now we add two eggs separately," she told us.

I think she meant 'separated' but that became apparent anyway.

With two small dishes in front of her, she hit the first egg with the edge of a knife and broke open the shell. It would seem that in her enthusiasm she had also broken the egg yolk so both egg and shells were put in one dish and removed to the back counter. Another small dish slowly slid into view on the right side of our television screen.

She successfully cracked a second egg, this time dropping the white into one of the little dishes, placing the yoke in the other. As she went through the same process with a second egg, a food mixer mysteriously shuffled into view on the left hand side of our screen.

Before picking up her wooden spoon, Elizabeth tipped the egg yolks into her lemon mixture and the egg whites into the Kenwood Chef bowl. She then went on to tell us something, although we had no idea what, because of the very loud motor and whizzing of beaters from the Kenwood which she had switched on to whip up the egg whites.

As she reached to turn off the machine we caught the tail end of her monologue.

"... cool down. Now we must add some sugar to the egg whites."

Delving back into the blue bucket she grabbed a handful or so of grains which she put into the egg whites before turning the machine back on and continuing to talk.

We tried to lip-read, but given that some of her words weren't exactly pronounced the same way as we would say them, this was a pretty pointless exercise.

Next she produced a jug of yellow stuff, which we assumed was a batch of the lemon concoction she had made earlier, and poured the thick substance into the precooked (and salted?) pastry case.

At last she turned off the food mixer, "… and now we place our egg whites on top of the tat" she said, spreading them evenly, "before cooking it in the oven for ten minutes."

At which point she stood tall, hands on hips, with a broad smile on her face, almost as if expecting a round of applause. After a few moments a camera followed her as she walked to her left until she was standing behind another table on which proudly stood a fully finished tat. It looked quite impressive.

"Ladies and Gentlemen, I would now like to introduce you to our dinner guests for tonight."

A new camera swung into action revealing four rather nervous looking people seated around a dining table. I recall there was one lady and three men, the names of whom escape me other than that I do remember one of the gentlemen was the recently appointed Deputy Ambassador for Switzerland. I don't know if it was because he hailed from a sun-starved European country, but he looked decidedly pale.

Brandishing a fancy cake slice, Elizabeth cut four large wedges of tat which she lifted carefully onto four small plates before passing them on to her guests.

"Please now," she smiled, "enjoy your tat."

With some reluctance the esteemed guests picked up their spoons as Elizabeth, the studio crew and probably 90% of Zambia's television-owning public watched with bated breath. As the guests gingerly tasted their tats, a look of some surprise appeared on their faces, and after his second spoonful the Swiss Ambassador spoke with a somewhat incredulous voice.

"Actually, this is quite nice," he said, and proceeded to polish off the lot.

Elizabeth beamed with delight at their enjoyment of her dish.

"Tell me Mr Ambassador, Sir, do you have anything like this in your country?" She asked.

"Indeed we do," answered the dignitary, "except we call it Lemon Meringue Pie."

"Yes, Sir," she replied, "that is what I said. *Lemon Frut Malingwe Tat!*"

We were never sure whether she had differentiation problems with her R's and L's, or if someone had spelled meringue incorrectly on her recipe card, but from that day to this, whenever I make Lemon Meringue Pie for my family or guests, it is always called a Lemon Melingwe Tat.

* * * * *

A few months later we were watching Elizabeth at work again when an uninvited guest appeared on the show.

I can't recall what she was making, to be honest the beginning of the show paled into insignificance after this, but once again she was making full use of her food mixer.

I didn't know if she was off doing something else but it appeared the cameraman and producer had either fallen asleep or gone off to the pub, because the camera was fully focused on the mixer, which took up the entire screen. Getting bored with watching the bowl swivelling round I was about to go and make a cup of tea when something caught my eye. It looked like a whisker. And it was waving from behind the Kenwood stand. Then a second one appeared. I stood mesmerised.

Then I realised that these weren't whiskers they were feelers, and they moved out from behind the stand followed by the body of a big fat cockroach!

Hubby had already begun to drift off to sleep in his chair,

"*Ziggy, wake up!*"

He sat bolt upright in his armchair, "What ...what ...?"

"Look at this!" I said, flapping my arm at the television.

"Bloody hell!"

The cockroach was now in full view, on the counter in front of the mixer stand. After a bit more feeler waving it backed up an inch or so and began exploring the base of the Kenwood with its feelers. Then it slowly began to ascend the mixer stand.

By this time a bomb might have exploded in our house and it would not have moved us from our vigil in front of the screen. Slowly the roach climbed up the machine, investigating the control knob with its sensitive antennae along the way. We were quite surprised by the bravery of the creature given the vibration which was given off by the machine. It eventually reached the summit and stood triumphantly on top of the mixer. The amount of time it spent lying there Ziggy reckoned it was getting some sort of a thrill from the vibrating appliance, but then that's typical of the way Ziggy's mind works.

Suitably rested from its long haul up the vertical stand, it now inched its way along the arm of the mixer. This section of course had even more movement than the base, having two beaters hurtling around at 300 rpm attached to the end of it.

We figured it was only a matter of time before the huge beastie was shaken off the shiny surface of the device and slid into the bowl, to be overwhelmed by whatever substance was being processed in there, and later presented to some unsuspecting diner on his tea plate.

Couldn't you just picture it?

And what if they had studio guests in that night, waiting to be served a tasty treat? They must have been turning green at the thought that it could be Cockroach Cake.

But the show rolled on. Amazingly, still clinging on with all six legs,

Roachie began to slowly move to the furthest side of the rocking mixer arm. Ziggy and I had stopped breathing some time before this. When we were convinced the creature was going to hurtle to a sticky demise, the television screen went blank.

At last we were able to draw breath even if we were exasperated by the sudden cessation of the excitement. A few more seconds elapsed before the Zambian Television Test Card appeared on the screen with an accompanying voice-over.

"This is an announcement. We are sorry for the loss of your picture due to a technical fault. There will now be a musical interlude."

"Yeah, technical fault. Right," we said in unison.

We reckoned that someone in a position of power must have woken up whilst watching the programme and managed to get hold of the studio, telling them to pull the plug pronto, either on the mixer, the camera, or the mains.

After a couple of minutes we were entertained by marching band music, undoubtedly the Zambian Military Band.

It didn't hold quite the same entertainment value.

And we never did find out what Elizabeth was making. We pooled a guess at Cockroach Crunchies.

II
All Hales Well for Christmas '82

During our second year in Zambia, I had made a new friend at the theatre. Her name was Jane Hales. She worked part-time at the theatre office, as the bar stock controller, and I would see her pottering about behind the bar whilst I was wandering around doing the various things that lured me to the place on an almost daily basis. Jane was half a generation older than I was and we got on like a house on fire. Her husband, Robin, worked for ZCCM, (the mine), and it transpired that they lived less than half a mile from us.

They had a pool and we were invited to go to their house whenever we wanted a swim during the hot summer days. Not only did they have a pool, they also had a sauna.

Monday nights, during winter, was when Jane and Robin would invite friends round to enjoy the sauna. Running from the steaming sauna and jumping into the cold pool on a winter's night was certainly very exhilarating.

There was never a question of having a sauna in the summer as the temperature of the pool water wouldn't have been cold enough to counter the heat of the sauna. Besides, the last thing you wanted to do at night was get hotter than you had already been all day.

Although everyone was modestly dressed in swimwear, we rarely took the children with us. We weren't sure it was the sort of thing kids should be doing, and even if there had been space, it would have been past their bedtime. Anyway, this gave Benton another opportunity to earn a bit of extra money, child-minding.

The Hales also had a couple of teenage kids but they were away at boarding school most of the time. They had originally been at boarding school in Zimbabwe but, as they reached senior level, Jane and Robin felt it was better for them to be schooled in the UK as they feared for their safety in Zimbabwe. Many people we knew, who worked for the mine, sent their children to boarding school either in the UK or South Africa, especially for senior schooling. At the time, private schooling in Zambia only catered for children up to age eleven.

Having been raised chiefly by my grandmother, Doris, whilst my mum and dad slogged away in her grocery business, I was determined that I would always be there for my kids, so boarding school for them was never going to be on the cards. My mum had told me after I got married that the one thing she regretted in life was not having spent much time with me as a child, although we did socialise together a lot as I got older.

The thing that has haunted me in later years is that I did not give her much opportunity to make up for that with her grandchildren. Instead I selfishly carted them thousands of miles away across the globe.

But where was I? Oh yes, the Hales family.

Having had a fairly quiet Christmas in 1981, the Christmas of 1982 was a totally different box of rabbits because Jane and Robin invited us to join them on Christmas Day. Knowing Jane, we knew it wouldn't be quiet. Whoever first used the phrase, 'laughed like a drain' must have met Jane!

We weren't the only ones accorded the privilege of an invitation. There was a whole crowd of people, most of whom we had previously met. A couple who had been their friends for years were known by everyone in Kitwe as Uncle Dick and Aunty Sylvia. They too were pretty active at the theatre, though not on stage. Uncle Dick was always the one to dress up as Santa Claus for any kiddies' Christmas parties, and this one was to be no exception.

Christmas day began as usual for us with the children anxious to get into the lounge to see if Santa had been whilst they were asleep, and shrieking with delight when they found presents stacked under the tree. A cup of tea and home-made shortbread had become our traditional Christmas breakfast, eaten as the kids excitedly unwrapped their gifts.

Then an early morning telephone call to my parents made the day extra special.

Next we collected all the food, drinks, and other goodies, to take to Jane and Robin's. This included gifts for Santa to hand out when he made his surprise visit.

All the guests had been asked to bring a gift, costing no more than two *kwacha*, which pretty much guaranteed that it would be something silly. And it had to be suitable for male or female recipients. The exception to this rule were the children's gifts, with each gift being named and the condition that we didn't 'go overboard'. Santa's sack was hidden in the garage where all these gifts were quietly deposited when the guests arrived.

With all preparations for the meal under control in the kitchen, we made sure that all the children were outside before calling the adults to join the impending festivities.

On the dot of three o'clock there came the sound of a ringing bell, distant but getting closer.

"What on earth is that noise?" called out Jane.

The seven children stood stock still, eyes wide, mouths agape, listening.

"Do you know what that is, Leon?"

"No."

"Where's Brad?"

"It's nothing to do with me," said Brad, walking from behind a table, "I'm here."

"Ho, ho, ho!" came a voice from the other side of a wall.

"It's Santa!" went up a cry from all the children, even the two who were old enough to know who Santa really was, but knew better than to spoil it for the youngsters.

78

"Ho, ho, HO!" said Santa again, as his head appeared above the garden wall.

Screeches and shouts went up as the kids raced around the pool to get closer to Santa who was now towered larger than life, on the other side of the wall, with his sack over his shoulder.

"Oh, what's this? What a long way down. I won't be able to climb down to give you your presents."

"Get a ladder!"

"Somebody get a ladder."

"Hold on Santa, don't go anywhere, we'll find a ladder," Brad called, racing towards the house. A step-ladder miraculously appeared from behind some of the parents.

Robin, assisted by three of the kids, carried the steps over to the wall where it was firmly placed for Santa to climb onto.

How Uncle Dick managed to manoeuvre himself over the wall, obviously from a similar step-ladder on the other side, whilst steadfastly hanging onto his sack of goodies was quite miraculous. But climb down he did, ho, ho, ho-ing until he reached a sturdy armchair which had been placed on the *stoep* for his comfort.

"So am I going to hear some singing, then?" Santa wanted to know.

There followed a couple of very loud choruses of *Jingle Bells* and *We Wish You a Merry Christmas*, before Santa put his arm up in the air for silence.

"Would anyone here like a present?"

Shouts of, "Yes, me!" and "Me, please!" and "Yes, please!" could be heard, and not just from the children, although only they were jumping up and down with excitement.

Slowly all the gifts were handed out, Santa calling for adults to come forward between calling the names of the children.

As the last of the adults collected their presents, Santa rose from his chair.

"Well, that's it then, I'd better be on my way."

One little boy, still standing by the pool, was fighting back his tears.

"Santa, I didn't get a present," he said with a sob.

It was Leon, trying very hard to control the quiver of his bottom lip.

"What?" shouted Santa. "No present? What's your name?"

"Leon," he said. And just so there would be absolutely no doubt about it, "Leon James Patras."

"Well, let me see..."

Santa stuck his head in the sack and his arms could be seen moving around inside the sack like they were chasing a rabbit. His head re-appeared, beard slightly askew, but in his hands was a brightly-wrapped gift.

"Would you look at this!" he said, "I just found this in the sack, and it has *your* name on it!"

Leon raced across to Santa and gave him a big hug before accepting his present with a smile that stretched from ear to ear. A big cheer went up and

Santa made his way out, this time via the kitchen door.

As the grown-ups unwrapped their presents, the humour typical of expats was apparent. Among the gifts there were a packet of cigarettes (up for barter as the recipient was a non-smoker); a tube of Colgate toothpaste (the only brand available in Zambia); a tin of baked beans; a second-hand book; an enamel mug; a hair brush (also up for barter from the bald receiver); pack of playing cards; a tin of brown shoe polish; and a toilet roll.

It was ironic that Ziggy got the toilet roll because the poor chap was still in the throes of a bout of dysentery he'd contracted only two days before. He would probably be spending more time in the bathroom than at the dining table that day.

The content of the Christmas repast was quite limited as the variety of commodities available in Zambia had improved very little over the past couple of years.

To be sure that all the guests fully understood what they would be enjoying on this special day, I had compiled a printed menu for the occasion.

CHRISTMAS MENU
December 25th 1982

First Course

Rather odorous creature hauled from the bottom of a lake on the end of a piece of wire, which has had its outer bits and guts removed (hopefully) and after heat treatment is swished around in some pink stuff and served on shredded plant matter.

Main Course

Amputated limb of carcosium porcus with incinerated hide.
Remains of a stiff bullock riddled with blubber
and rolled in some stinking bits of vegetation
(purported to ward off mosquitoes and vampires).
Winged, though flightless, castrated creature suitably scorched.
Biggish, white things with crispy exterior previously
found under several inches of dirt.
Long, pointy colourful objects.
Medium sized green spheres from Western Europe
White blobs of organic matter vaguely resembling brains.
Lightly steamed Cerebrum Verde
Staff of Life blasted to Kingdom Come and soaked in
flavoured bovine excretion which is cooked to
the consistency of thick wallpaper paste.

A squishy mixture of wheat based fodder and
random vegetation shoved up the ass of meat.
A thickened liquid in which the innards of meat have
been boiled, then coloured to a crappy brown shade.

Dessert

A dark brown sticky, stodgy substance riddled with
revived dehydrated small fruit.
Small crusty objects crammed with mushed up stuff similar to above.
A pourable coagulated mass, resembling liquid banana skins,
which had been impregnated with a specific alcohol.
Seriously hot H2O which has been infused with brown particles
which may be served with various additives.
An interesting array of leave-me-legless refreshments
will be made available throughout.

WE DO HOPE YOU ENJOY YOUR MEAL

(I can't imagine why, but several people seemed a little reluctant to be
seated at our grand table in readiness for such a feast. Fortunately, on the
other side of the menu I had incorporated an interpretation.)

Fish Cocktail on a bed of Lettuce
Roast Leg of Pork with Crispy Crackling
Larded Fillet of Beef with Garlic
Roast Chicken (capon)
Roast Potatoes
Carrots
Brussels Sprouts
Cauliflower
Broccoli
Bread Sauce
Stuffing
Gravy
Christmas Pudding
Mince Pies
Brandy Custard
Liqueur Coffee
Wine will be served throughout the meal.

It was quite a long dinner, followed by more than a few guests crashing out
for postprandial snoozes. Once everyone had recovered, the celebration

continued with vast quantities of alcohol being consumed as the party progressed well into the night with silly games, the most entertaining being that of charades.

All in all, a jolly good time was had by all.

Some months later, Jane went back to the UK for good. I thought she had simply gone on long leave but then she didn't return. Only after many years did I find out why.

One evening she and Robin went out for supper with a couple of friends. They had gone to the Squash Club, renowned for its restaurant, and at the end of a most enjoyable meal they dropped their friends off. When they arrived home at their own gate, dark figures appeared from some nearby bushes and held them up at gunpoint. They stole their jewellery, money and made off in Robin's company car.

One thing they stole which could not be replaced, was Jane's love for living in Zambia. She chose to return permanently to the UK.

I missed my friend very much. Jane was always the life and soul of the party, but inside she was a very sensitive lady, so I can understand the fear this would have embedded in her. The sort of people who carried guns in Zambia were invariably inexperienced in their use; add to that their lack of respect for life and you have a very dangerous combination. I think it is as well I didn't know about this incident until much later, after we had left the country.

12

Enter the Land Rover

As 1983 progressed, things were getting busy at Rhinestone and, as Ziggy found that he could rely more extensively on Peter to do assorted jobs, the company car became increasingly less available to me. It was time to set me up with my own transport.

It is hard to convey just how difficult such a simple task as buying a secondhand car in Zambia was at that time. There simply weren't any. If people had a car that worked, they kept it until it was falling to bits. Such was the state of some of the vehicles in Zambia that some people kept theirs on the road well beyond that point.

Secondhand car dealerships were non-existent, and new vehicles only appeared when some company imported a convoy of Japanese cars, invariably all spoken for even before they crossed the border.

Then we heard about the Land Rover factory. Apparently they had set up a facility somewhere in Ndola, the other main city on the Copperbelt. They recovered old Land Rovers, took them to bits, then reassembled them, using any available replacement parts. The 'new' vehicle was then sold.

What a splendid idea, we thought . *We'll have one of those please.*

Ziggy tracked down their sales office and enquired about placing an order.

"Land Rover Zambia, good morning," said an English sounding gentleman, "how may I help you?"

"I'd like to buy a Land Rover please," said Ziggy.

"Certainly Sir. Depending on the specifications you require, the waiting time is approximately three months for a Land Rover Series 3. Are you happy with that?"

"Well, I guess I'll have to be."

"Excellent, Sir. If I could just take some particulars of your requirements..."

Ziggy waited as he heard the opening and closing of filing cabinet drawers, and shuffling of papers.

"Right Sir, what sort of Land Rover would you be requiring?"

"Well, what sort have you got?"

"We can put together virtually any combination of whatever you like, Sir."

"Could you perhaps give me a clue as to what's on offer?"

Ziggy was getting rather bored with the lack of direction.

"Perhaps we should start with the size, Sir. Would you like short wheelbase or long wheelbase?"

Ziggy thought about how much stuff I pack when we go for a Sunday outing with the kids.

"Long wheelbase, I think."

"Petrol or Diesel engine? Four or six cylinder?"

That took a little thought but petrol was more readily available than diesel fuel.

"Four cylinder petrol would do, thank you."

"Now would Sir like a soft-top? If so would this be a full soft-top or a hard-top cab with soft-top rear, or perhaps even a detachable hard-top rear? Or would Sir simply prefer a long wheelbase hard top?"

"Oh definitely a full-on hardtop. We have three kids."

"And would that be with roof-lights or without? "

"I beg your pardon?"

"In the roof Sir. They are like shallow windows in the top/side angle of the roof."

"No, I don't think we need those."

"And would you like three or five doors?

"Ummm…"

"Rear seats or open space? Perhaps Sir would just like some side storage boxes which could also be used for seating?"

"Er, yes."

"If only two doors, how many side windows would Sir like, and would they be fixed or opening windows?"

"I hadn't realised there would be such a choice."

"Then would Sir be requiring any externals, a roof-rack, front-winch or tow-bar?"

"Well, I don't…"

"And how many spare wheels would Sir like? We have spare wheel fixings on the bonnet, rear door, inside or undercarriage."

"I'll have to think about…"

"Yes, and Sir doesn't need to tell me what colour he wants the coachwork at this time."

"Oh, but I know the answer to that," Ziggy proudly proffered, "my wife wants a yellow one."

"Come again, Sir?"

"A yellow one. My wife is going to be the one using it most and says she wants a yellow one."

"Right. Any particular shade of yellow? Like egg yellow, or sunflower yellow, or telephone-yellow?"

Telephone-yellow related to the colour of the logo of the Zambian telephone company.

"I don't know. She didn't say. But she wants cloth seats."

"Cloth seats?"

"Yes, cloth seats. She says plastic seats make her bum sweat."

"Cloth seats it is, Sir. Any particular colour for those?"

"Oh, I don't think it matters, as long as they're cloth."

"Right Sir. So we have established that Sir would like a long wheelbase, 4 cylinder petrol engine, Series 3 Land Rover, with hardtop (no roof-lights) and fixed side windows, internal storage boxes and painted yellow. With cloth seats, of course, Sir."

"Er, yes."

"Then if Sir would give me his name and phone number I shall keep a note of Sir's preliminary order until such time as Sir can give me a little more information as to the other requirements."

These initial formalities completed, Ziggy put down the phone with the feeling that he had just made a complete and utter idiot of himself.

The following few days we scrutinised every Land Rover we saw. After some discussion we eventually refined our requirements and placed the final order with Land Rover, forwarding a deposit. We also confirmed that it should be painted telephone-yellow, have a black interior and, of course, have cloth seats.

After a few weeks we received a call, saying, because of our somewhat unusual request, they were having a problem sourcing suitably durable fabric for cloth seats. Would we be happy with dralon?

Having had a gold-corded dralon lounge suite in the UK, which we loved, I was quite happy with that.

We then sat back and waited for our vehicle. And waited. And waited.

We eventually got a call, two days before we were due to go on leave to the UK, that it was ready for collection. The following morning Peter and I drove through to Ndola to collect a nice 'new' Land Rover.

When we arrived at the factory we found that it wasn't quite finished. They were in the middle of fitting a second wing-mirror and also needed to 'touch-up' some paintwork.

We drove off for an hour to see if there was anything interesting happening in Ndola, (there wasn't), before returning to be told that all was ready.

After completing the necessary paperwork, with Malcolm the Sales Manager, I was escorted outside to be introduced to our new acquisition. As we rounded the side of the building, there she stood in all her splendour, our new yellow-ish Land Rover.

"Nice, isn't she?" said Malcolm, proudly waving his hand at what he thought would be my dream on four wheels.

I gulped.

"Lovely," I murmured.

It wasn't quite the shade of yellow I had in mind. Actually, I wasn't really sure if it was yellow. Malcolm, or his coach-builder manager, had obviously seen a different coloured 'telephone-yellow' logo to the one I knew. Perhaps it had been a faded one.

Without a paint box it is difficult to describe the shade of colour. Let us just say that if one stood it next to something green, it looked yellow. But if you stood it next to something yellow, it looked a pale green. So it was a sort of yellowy-green.

With a sigh of resignation, which Malcolm mistook as one of contentment, I moved to take a closer look at this mechanical masterpiece. With a flourish, or as far as one can flourish the opening of a Land Rover door, he exposed the interior of the cab.

Now I seriously could not believe my eyes. There, in all their glory, were my cloth covered seats, upholstered in a glaring **candy pink** dralon!

I was speechless.

"We had a devil of a job tracking down that fabric for your seats," he announced with a beaming smile of satisfaction.

"Yes, I bet you did," I responded. "It isn't *quite* the colour I had expected."

Malcolm continued to beam and took me on a guided tour of my new acquisition.

Lifting the bonnet he revealed a spotless, shining engine. Except for the battery, radiator cap, and dip stick, it meant nothing to me. We walked around, examining the petrol cap and rear door. He opened the latter to reveal two rows of fixed metal boxes, running the length of each side of the interior, and which the kids would use as seats.

He then invited me to get in the driver's seat whilst he pointed out the items on the incredibly basic dashboard. I didn't think I would have much trouble getting to grips with those!

What I thought I might have trouble with, though, was the gearstick. It looked about six feet long and, when selecting gears, had a span which stretched to arms' length. Thankfully I have pretty long arms for a woman.

I toyed with this for a few moments before Malcolm pointed to a short lever with an oval knob on it. It sat dwarfed beneath the main gearstick.

"And here is your four-wheel-drive engager," he said.

Four-wheel-drive? What the hell did I want with four-wheel-drive? Come to that, what the hell did I want with a bloody Land Rover?

Honestly, I must have been one of the biggest twits of all time. I didn't even realise that all Land Rovers had four-wheel-drive. Talk about an idiot!

I fiddled around with that, knowing full well I'd forget everything he told me by the time I reached home.

After a minute or so, Malcolm made a polite, attention-grabbing cough.

"I really hate to rush you, but I do have some paperwork to finish off in the office and the factory will be closing in 20 minutes…"

I duly stopped fiddling around and started the engine. It worked. Malcolm then handed me the spare key, shook my hand and wished me happy driving.

"There is enough petrol in the tank to get you to the nearest petrol station," he added, almost as an afterthought, "which is about 5 kilometres along the Kitwe road."

During this time, Peter had been standing by taking this all in.

"I'll lead the way to the petrol station," he said, "then once we're back on the road I'll have to dash off to collect the boss."

As I drove behind Peter, I reflected on a few conversations I'd recently had with friends. When they found out I was getting a Land Rover they'd ask if I had ever driven one before. On admitting that I had not, the response was always the same, they would collapse into heaps of laughter. Now I knew why.

All I can say is that it was a good job that I'd been going to keep-fit classes during the previous few weeks. And I soon realised why it had such a large steering wheel. I would have arms the size of a wrestler's in no time at all.

It wasn't long before Peter turned into the BP garage. I pulled up at one of the pumps and first checked that I had sufficient cash before asking the attendant to fill her up. I settled down in the driver's seat and tried to look like a seasoned Land Rover driver sitting on her pink dralon upholstery. As was the norm, the pumping of petrol was a laboriously slow procedure.

After several minutes I was startled from my reverie.

"Stop, stop, stop, *stop!* Hey you, *stop!*" Peter was screaming and running across the forecourt towards the pumps. The attendant looked up to see what the fuss was about.

"Stop pumping that petrol!" yelled Peter.

The attendant stopped. I jumped out of my seat to find out what on earth was the matter. Peter got down on his knees and looked under the Land Rover.

"Look at this," he said, and pointed out a rapidly expanding wet patch on the ground.

I crouched and peered beneath my 'brand-new' vehicle to see petrol piddling from the fuel tank onto the tarmac.

"*Damn!* We'd better get this thing back to the factory, and quickly, before they close," I said. "There is *no way* we're taking this to Kitwe."

I tore across to the service station kiosk to pay for the fuel, insisting on a receipt for the records. This seemed to take forever as it had to be hand-written. Then, with Peter following behind me for safety's sake, we raced back to the Land Rover factory.

But there wasn't much racing to be done as we couldn't exit onto the main road. I had never seen so much traffic in Zambia before. I think every vehicle in Ndola (including its surrounding areas) must have been on that particular road on that particular afternoon.

Some kind soul eventually let us out and we sped back to the factory. Just as I was approaching the entrance, a car turned out of the gates. It was Malcolm.

"Malcolm! Malcolm! Stop!" I shouted and tried to beep the horn, but couldn't find it.

Behind me Peter was taking similar measures, except he succeeded in making much more noise than I had. And for good measure he slewed the company Fiat in front of Malcolm's car, rather like a police roadblock. That got his attention. We quickly explained the problem and we all drove back inside the factory gates.

While Malcolm was filling out the paperwork, to take return of the vehicle, I took the opportunity to list the additional faults I had already noticed.

"I know I'm no expert in these things, but I would like to say that I thought the steering was incredibly loose. I turned the wheel a good four inches before I could feel any movement kicking in. Also, the brakes aren't very good. I had to push my foot almost to the floor to slow it down. And, when I was waiting at the petrol station, I noticed some paint flaking off the passenger door. Surely that isn't right on such a 'new' Land Rover?"

I was on a roll.

"And talking of the passenger door, it doesn't want to stay open. When I opened it wide, to reach inside to get money from my purse, the damn thing closed on me and nearly amputated my legs!"

I finished with a scowl.

"Oh dear," Malcolm sighed. "Don't worry, I'll get all those things sorted out for you but it might take a couple of days.

"Never mind a couple of days," I told him, "you can take a couple of weeks to make sure it's all sorted properly. We're off on holiday tomorrow. I'll call you, when we get back, to arrange for its collection."

At which I turned on my heels and Peter and I beat a hasty retreat back to Kitwe. I could imagine Ziggy tearing his hair out, waiting for Peter to pick him up.

As it happened I needn't have worried because he'd already figured out that something was delaying us and had hitched a lift to the Club with someone else. The kids, of course, were most disappointed to find that we didn't have our new toy.

13
Never Travel Solo with Kids

As we had approached the school summer holidays, I had to arrange for Brad to be seen once again by an ENT specialist about his ears. Grommets were still needed to counter the 'glue ear' problem he had been experiencing for the past couple of years and, as surgery for this still wasn't available in Zambia, it once more necessitated a trip to the UK.

Whilst we flew back as a family, work issues demanded that Ziggy return to Zambia after two weeks. The kids and I would follow a few days later once Brad had been given the 'all clear' after new grommets had been inserted.

I look back on that journey with mixed feelings. As actual flights go it was perfectly smooth, but I can hardly confess to actually having enjoyed some of the accompanying experiences. The first leg from East Midlands down to Heathrow was uneventful as the kids sat quietly looking out of the windows and didn't have time to get bored. After that it went, as Ziggy predicted, downhill.

On arrival at Heathrow we trooped along to the baggage collection point and after quite a long wait found and loaded all our stuff onto two trolleys. I tried using only one but four suitcases and four lots of cabin baggage saw at least one bag tumbling off every couple of paces.

When I had spoken with Ziggy, the day before our departure, he had assured me that it would be a straightforward passage through Heathrow.

"Just follow the signs," he'd said, "it's all downhill. Unlike when we travelled in the opposite direction when we flew in."

On that journey we didn't have full cases, and there were two adults.

"You'll manage it just fine," he said.

We were okay for the first three miles (that's what it seemed like) as the ground was pretty flat. Then we came to the ramp. I say 'ramp' because that is what the airport called it. Personally I thought it bore a closer resemblance to a slalom ski run.

I stood at the top and surveyed the slopes with the keen eye of an engineer's wife and worked out that the first leg of about eight yards had a gradient of about 1 in 3. Then it levelled for as long as it took to turn a 90° corner onto a half landing of about 4 yards. There it turned on another 90° after which it carried on down another 1 in 3 for a further eight yards.

I went first, leaving Vicki and Leon with Brad at the top of the ramp, who was in charge of the second trolley containing the cabin baggage.

Only once I started down the slope did I try to apply the brake, and realised the error of not testing it first. Despite a white-knuckle vice-like grip, the brake had absolutely no effect at all upon the increasing momentum of the trolley. Brad wouldn't stand a cat in hell's chance.

Leaning back on my dug-in heels I turned to shout a warning to the kids to stay where they were but they were already on their way.

Trolley number two was coming diagonally towards me. Slowly at first, then, with the added weight of three screaming kids, who were all clinging to it like limpets, it picked up impetus.

"Mummy, this is FUN!" they shouted as they hurtled towards me at about 50 mph.

A few valuable seconds passed as I tried to decide which way to jump. I settled instead on an attempt to try to stop it, which sort of worked in that it didn't kill me or crash into my trolley, but did result in the entire contents of that trolley spilling onto the floor, together with a tangle of kids.

As they rolled about in fits of hysterical laughter, I stood back to mop my brow and looked up to see an elderly Indian couple standing at the top of the ramp, a look of sheer horror on their faces, as they had obviously envisaged a total write-off of a young family.

After we had re-loaded the trolleys, and I had convinced Brad that this was not the Heathrow version of the big dipper (a roller coaster), the elderly couple very kindly offered their assistance and helped with the second trolley as we continued down the second Heathrow ski-slope.

We parted company with the lovely people when they diverted to the railway station which apparently was situated somewhere beneath Terminal 3. Then we faced the moving pavements.

Brad, being once again in charge of trolley number two, attempted to beat the world record trolley speed along the conveyor belt, crashing into the sides every few yards. After much shouting and resorting to sending messages via Vicki and Leon he did eventually park up at one of the static intervals.

I then took charge of both trolleys. As I played 'pull me/push you' with the two trolleys, Brad then attempted the world speed record at running the wrong way along this human conveyor belt.

I was quite relieved when we reached the end of this string of airport conveniences only to be presented by another challenge.

I should never have believed Ziggy.

Within sight of the terminal building, to which we were headed, we arrived at yet another ramp. Only this time it was steeper and going *up*. I was already absolutely exhausted so we waited a few minutes at the foot of the ramp whilst I built myself up to it.

Taking a very deep breath I charged this ramp with everything I could muster. I got about three-quarters of the way up before I was forced to slow down to a long-strided shove, when I thought I heard voices behind me. I turned to see all three kids a third of the way up the ramp with the second trolley, which was on the point of deciding it preferred to be at the bottom.

A finishing spurt on my part got my trolley full of suitcases to the top of the ramp before I turned and frantically raced back down. It was a close call, but I was able to grab the errant trolley just as it had started to roll back onto the three squawking kids. By this time I was wheezing like a ninety-year-old chain-smoker finishing a marathon.

In a state of almost total collapse I managed to push the second trolley the rest of the way up the ramp whilst shouting at the kids to run up to the top to 'mind' the first trolley. It happened to be standing by an open door with my handbag containing tickets, passports, money, etc sitting in plain view on top of the cases.

I suppose you'd expect the rest of the journey to be uneventful after that lot.

Really?

By the time we sauntered through the terminal to departures we arrived at the Zambia Airways check-in desk at 4:30. It needed half an hour to open, so I parked the trolleys to be first in line, then we all sat on the floor and waited for 5:00. The kids even sat quietly.

Check-in was a dream, with all bags being within the required weight limit, and we even had first choice in seats. As was my preference, I opted for the very back row of the Boeing 707 and the kind lady said that, as the flight wasn't showing full, she would try to keep the remaining two of the six seats empty so that we could spread out.

We then made our way through passport control and had our cabin bags x-rayed for goodness knows what. The guys at the machine could not figure out Brad's bag and unpacked it to find a large shoe box crammed very carefully with his collection of cars and lorries. The bloke who inspected it obviously had children of his own because he chatted easily with Brad who amazingly was not at all fazed by having his precious collection disturbed. And I will hand it to the guy, he repacked it beautifully once he'd established there was no Action Man in the bag with an AK47.

We eventually arrived at the departure lounge and I decided to get the chores over and done with. I deposited the kids on some seats, together with the bags and threats of almost certain death if they left them, and went off to the duty free shop.

During the phone call I'd had with Ziggy, he had instructed me to buy a two-litre bottle of whisky, saying that the Zambian customs chaps in Lusaka are so dippy that, whilst they know you are only allowed to bring one bottle of spirits into the country, they never question the size of the bottle.

I then moved onto the perfume counter and, having treated myself to my favourite potion, was on my way to buy a couple of roller-ball pen refills from WH Smith when I got a feeling of foreboding. I could hear a noise which sounded awfully like my kids having a lot of fun.

As I headed back to the lounge area I could see they were having a whale of a time, running along a row of seats then dive-bombing over the back and onto the adjoining row of seats, doing their versions of the Fosbury Flop. Strange how this row of seats had miraculously emptied of other humans since I'd left the kids there.

Having lowered myself from the ceiling, I stormed across and grabbed the three of them in a none too gentle manner and deposited them unceremoniously on the seats in a manner for which the seats were intended. From their reactions I think they had gathered pretty fast that maybe this time they had gone a little too far.

"If I hear that any of you have spoken to each other, touched each other or even looked at each other, or moved one fraction of an inch whilst I'm gone, you will get a severe beating. *Do you understand me?*"

"Yes, Mummy," came the multiple, meek reply. And I returned to finish my shopping.

It was with considerable relief that I heard the announcement that our flight was now boarding at Gate 47 and we went forward in an orderly fashion to the plane.

For a change, they had a policy of 'families with children first' and as our seats were right at the back we were the first to board. And as promised, we had the row to ourselves.

Vicki sat by the window on the left, with a couple of bags in the middle seat and me in the aisle seat. Brad sat by the window on the right with Leon sitting in the middle, trying to peer over Brad's shoulder to look through the window. My plan was to move across to sit next to Leon once dinner was served, and then bring Vicki into my vacated seat so that they were all nicely at hand for having food sorted out. Once that was over I could stretch Brad and Leon out on one row, leaving the other side for Vicki and me.

We were taxiing to the end of the runway when all of a sudden a bod, who incidentally had earlier been wandering up and down the aisle, plonked his bag down on the seat next to Leon. I looked up in astonishment and for want of anything else, said, "Oh!".

The bloke looked at me as he unsuccessfully tried to cram his bag into the overhead locker.

"This isn't anyone's seat is it?" he asked.

"Well, no, but ..."

"Oh, good!" he said and sat himself down.

"I was given a middle seat further up the plane but didn't have enough leg room."

As if that explained everything.

I rapidly pointed out that I couldn't possibly be separated from the two children. As I needed to supervise their meals, he'd have to move over to the window seat once the plane had taken off. I impressed upon him that the children were terribly active, would be up and down all the time, and could only sleep lying down.

He was not to be moved.

"I don't mind if they put their head or feet on me," he said, "and I'll help them when they need help."

Oh, great! I thought, *that's all we need. A damned martyr!*

As soon as we'd taken off, and the seat belt sign had been switched off, I muttered, "Okay, let's get this show on the road."

I looked to my left to find that Vicki and already fallen asleep, then to Leon to find he was asleep also. Brad was still awake, but horror of horrors, the bloke sitting in the aisle seat was also asleep.

"Er, we'll change round now, when you're ready," I said to him.

Nothing.

I repeated myself somewhat louder but the fool slept on.

He eventually raised an eyelid when the dinner trolley was about two rows away. We then had to have him get out of his seat, followed by Brad, then the bloke had to climb over the still sleeping Leon to get into the window seat. Then came the passing over of his bag which, to give him more leg room, I agreed could be put on the floor in front of Leon (though why the hell I should've been so accommodating was beyond me). I got Brad settled into his aisle seat just as the Air Hostess's bottom came between us.

Brad and I quite enjoyed our meals though I did pass on the dessert which was a rather ghastly looking piece of chocolate cake which felt about as heavy as my first attempt at making bread. After a couple of drinks and the removal of the dinner trays, I contorted my body to lie down in the aisle and centre seats. I was about to fade into oblivion when, yes, you've guessed it, Vicki and Leon woke up.

Then they were up and down, up and down, wandering into the galley to scrounge food, looking for things to do, all very limited as I'm sure you can imagine.

They did eventually settle down and by some miracle I managed to get a couple of hours sleep before the morning breakfast ritual began.

We landed in Lusaka at 6:00am and, whilst I'll never know how I did it, we were amongst the first off the plane. Consequently we were the first to check in for the onward flight to Kitwe so we all had our own seats (unlike the very first journey we had taken to Kitwe more than three years earlier).

I miraculously managed to secure a trolley, as those were like gold dust in Lusaka airport. As we loaded all our bags onto it I recalled Ziggy's instructions in his phone call.

"When you go through customs you have to present yourself and your cases to a customs official at a long wooden bench-like counter. The best thing is to declare a certain amount of innocent sounding stuff, to satisfy their curiosity, pay the duty on it then get your cases to the Kitwe baggage check-in."

Simple.

One of our suitcases was amongst the last to appear, but while I was waiting for that I'd at least had time to fill in the customs declaration form. Pushing the precariously packed trolley, we made our way through to the slowly emptying customs hall.

I decided I might as well pretend ignorance and tootled up to the kiosk, where one pays one's dues, and handed over my form in the hope the man would tell me how much to pay. It was only then that I noticed others had had their forms filled in and signed by a customs official, stating how much duty was due.

I realised that I would probably be turned away and parked the trolley and kids near the exit, before returning to the customs man by the bench-counter.

"How much do I need to pay on this?" I asked.

"But where are your cases?"

"Over there, by those three children," I said innocently.

He pointed to another customs official standing between our trolley and the pay kiosk.

"Go to the man over there," he said, then turned his back on me.

Being the naïve sort of person I am (tee hee) I went to the kiosk instead, and when it was my turn, asked how much I had to pay.

"You must see that man over there," the money man said, pointing to the bloke I'd just left.

"Oh, he sent me over here," I replied, looking all innocent like.

"That's okay then," he responded, and proceeded to calculate the amount of duty due.

I was pretty impressed with myself for having avoided having my cases opened, which contained far more new and interesting stuff than was on my form.

"That will be K30.45n," he said.

I enquired if I could pay by cheque, to which he replied that I could, as long as it was in *kwacha*.

I got my cheque book from my bag on the trolley, which had been abandoned by the kids and who were now running up and down the counters, and wrote out the cheque, omitting the payee.

"Who do I make it out to?" I enquired of the cashier.

"Oh, is it a personal cheque?" he said, peering down at my cheque book. "We don't accept those. I thought you meant Travellers' Cheques.

I told him that I didn't have any Travellers Cheques left and that the only *kwacha* cash I had was the K10 we were allowed to take out of the country.

"Haven't you got any change?"

I dug around in the bottom of my bag and found 40 *ngwe* (the equivalent of cents).

"That will do," he said, crossing out the initial K34.45 on the form and inserting the much smaller K10.40.

I was still chuckling to myself when we reached the gate at domestic departures.

Ziggy will be proud of me, I thought.

The final one-hour leg of the journey was remarkably uneventful and at nine o'clock we landed in Kitwe in brilliant sunshine.

As I walked across the tarmac I must have looked like I'd spent the night in a sewer, but that didn't stop me from getting a big hug from my lovely husband who was waiting for us by the security gate.

We were all very happy to be home.

* * * * *

Having thoroughly enjoyed our holiday, I was now looking forward to becoming fully mobile. I tried for three days before I was eventually able to get through on the telephone to Land Rover. When I did, it was to find that Malcolm wasn't there and I was connected to a Manager named Mr Warburton.

I asked him if he was conversant with our situation and, rather tartly, he replied that he was and that the vehicle had been awaiting collection for the past two months. Before I could utter a word, he continued his snotty tirade.

"What is more, one of your earlier cheques bounced!"

"Okay, stop right there, please," I demanded.

Clearly he did not know what the devil he was talking about. I told him that Malcolm had been made fully aware that we would only be collecting the vehicle after we returned from holiday and rattled off all the faults which had been found when I first picked it up. I pointed out that I had a receipt for forty litres of fuel that had been filled into the faulty tank and the vehicle had better have as much when we collected it this time.

I was on a roll.

"Furthermore, I think you ought to take a look at your Accounts Department. It doesn't say much for their efficiency if they let us take possession of a vehicle with K6000.00 outstanding on the payment!"

I could almost see his face turning red on the other end of the telephone.

He apologised for his obvious misunderstanding of the situation, blaming it on 'mistaken identity' (contradicted of course by the K6000 shortfall). I asked him about the 'duff' cheque.

Evidently it was one made out by Rhinestone (a bit scary, being Ziggy's employer) so I told him to return it to me immediately and I would bring along a bank-certified cheque when I collected the Land Rover.

It was over a week before the duff cheque arrived. One of Rhinestone's office chappies was sent to collect a banker's draft from the bank and take it to Ziggy's office. But, upon leaving the bank, he was set upon by five armed robbers who relieved him of his briefcase containing a fair bit of cash and, yes, you guessed it, the banker's draft.

It was Monday before we could organise yet another replacement cheque.

Once again, Peter and I set off for Ndola, this time with three very excited children in the back seat. At the Land Rover factory I was greeted by a very sugary Mr Warburton, who led me out to the yard, and once again I was presented with my 'new' vehicle. It hadn't changed colour. It was still a vague yellow/green shade of indecision.

I checked out all the bits which I had previously found fault with and all seemed to be in order. Mr Warburton assured me that the petrol tank was 'full to overflowing'.

"I certainly hope it isn't, this time," I said, which of course went completely over his fat head.

At a nod from me, Brad, Vicki and Leon leapt out of the car where they had been waiting, fit to burst, and raced over to inspect their new toy. As they clambered in the back they were thrilled to find that they could actually walk around inside.

Oh dear. I could foresee trouble ahead and threatened them all, there and then, that if any one of them so much as thought about walking around during the journey, they would soon find themselves walking outside the vehicle, all the way back to Kitwe. They did behave, well, pretty much.

The return drive was quite sedate, with Peter following behind. There were a couple of dodgy moments when it nearly died, perhaps from a problem with water in the fuel tank, or some such oddity.

During the course of the journey we decided that our new vehicle must have a name. We didn't want to keep calling it 'the Land Rover'. After tossing aside Smokie, Kit, Doogle, Kermit, Fozzie, and various other television personalities suggested by the children, we settled on Lizzy.

As we neared home I found that it was becoming increasingly difficult to turn the steering wheel when cornering. When I pulled up outside our gate, and tooted the horn to be let in, Peter arrived behind me and was pointing at something. I jumped out of the cab, walked round the front and was just in time to see the nearside front tyre sink the last couple of centimetres into the ground. Lizzy had a puncture!

Apparently, about half a mile from home, Peter noticed it was slowly deflating and prayed that it would last until we got there. I carefully inched it inside our garden until Peter had enough space to pass through in the car.

He then turned his attention to the nice new spare wheel, which was fixed to the rear door. We then discovered that our custom-built vehicle apparently did not come equipped with a jack or wheel-brace.

Oh the joys of living in Zambia!

14
Spotlight on Lizzy

If you think we'd already had a few problems with Lizzy, then, quoting the lyrics of the Bachman Turner Overdrive song, *You Ain't Seen Nothin' Yet.*

On the evening of the day we'd collected Lizzy I opened my handbag to discover that, in all the excitement, I'd forgotten to give the new banker's draft to Mr Warburton. I spent the next couple of days trying to reach him and persuaded him to send somebody to come fetch it. When their representative collected the cheque he asked if Lizzy was working okay.

"It's difficult to say, actually," I told him. "Due to it taking us almost three days to find a wheel-brace and jack to fix a puncture, I've only driven it about ten kilometres, so it hasn't really had time to go wrong yet."

Talk about 'famous last words'!

During the following two days a couple of journeys across town saw it doing the Lizzy Fade on several occasions. Perseverance and a lot of patience eventually saw it re-start. We found that it started perfectly when the engine was cold, but once it warmed up it was a different matter.

On the Sunday we had arranged to meet a bunch of friends at Mindola Dam, a popular leisure spot. Of course, me being my usual shy self, I insisted on showing off by arriving in grand style in Lizzy. Except that we didn't.

At the entrance we had to confirm that our friends had booked us in, and when we came to a stop so did the engine. I tried persistently to re-start it as a queue of cars began building up behind us. Eventually we resorted to getting a bunch of people to push us out of the way. We locked up and walked to where our friends were waiting for us. Not quite the grand entrance I'd had in mind.

Half an hour later Ziggy went and tried again and successfully brought Lizzy round to where we all were, and we were able to enjoy our own cold beers instead of scrounging off everyone else. Being the naïve idiots that we were, we still put this problem down to water in the petrol tank.

On Monday Brad had afternoon activities (compulsory extra schooling) which Ziggy normally took him to on his way back to work after lunch. This week he decided to leave early, leaving me to take Brad in Lizzy. To add to the madness, all three kids had been invited to a birthday party and I was still in the middle of making the birthday girl a dress as her gift. At 13:55 I had to stop to take Brad to Lechwe School. Lizzy performed without a hitch.

By 14:45 I was done, and packed Vicki and Leon, together with the new dress, into Lizzy and set off to collect Brad before depositing them all at the party. We got as far as the end of our road where I had to halt at the T-junction. Lizzy quietly died. After fruitless attempts to re-start, I spotted a car coming towards us, driven by an expat woman. I flagged her down and asked if she would be kind enough to drive back to our house and tell Benton and our gardener that I needed help.

She not only did that, she also returned with them and, on hearing that I was on my way to collect my son from Lechwe, kindly offered to do the honours as she was going there to fetch her own kids. I didn't know the woman from Adam, but one didn't worry about that sort of thing in our environment.

As the unknown lady went off with my two youngest kids, who could identify their brother waiting at Lechwe, Benton and Clement attempted to push Lizzy, backwards, to our house. After about twenty yards the poor chaps were melting from the effort and I told them to give up. I left Clement guarding the lifeless machine and Benton and I walked back home.

It may sound odd to you that I left the gardener guarding a defunct Land Rover. I assure you this was a necessity. Any vehicle left untended on the roadside was likely to be relieved of its battery and all the wheels in no time at all. I know, I know, the week before it took us three days to replace a flat tyre. But believe me, the 'right people' in Zambia would have all four wheels off faster than a Formula One pit team, using nothing more than a screwdriver and a few lumps of rock.

Your next question might be, *why didn't you phone Ziggy and ask him to send a mechanic?*

Therein lies the next obstacle. You see, our telephone had been out of order all day, so I couldn't phone *anyone*.

I waited in the garden with a cold beer until the strange woman returned with my kids. I thanked her profusely for her kindness, whereupon she said it was entirely her pleasure, especially 'meeting such delightful children'. I wondered if it was ours or someone else's kids she was talking about.

The kids and I then walked down the road to the party, which was only six houses away, where I was able to use my friend's phone to call Ziggy and ask him to send help, before walking back home. Half an hour later Peter arrived with some non-mechanical bod.

We drove up the road to where Lizzy still sat under the watchful eyes of Clement. I said I'd have one last try at starting it before they towed it back to our house. Naturally it started first time, so I reversed my way along Frazer Crescent and parked it once more in our garden.

After discussing our predicament with a few pals it was decided that the coil was at fault. The next morning Ziggy followed me round to the Theatre where I parked up and he went off to a work meeting nearby before buying and returning with a new coil. After removing the original and installing the replacement, he discovered that he had two wires left over and decided it would be a good time to fetch a Rhinestone mechanic.

As soon as Ziggy arrived with the mechanic, I took Ziggy's car to do my shopping, returning well over an hour later to find a frustrated pair awaiting my return in order that they might go and get an auto electrician. On their return I reclaimed the car again so that I could take home my rapidly thawing chickens and collect the kids and some fodder for what looked like a long session at the Club.

As I drove back into the car park, I met the mechanic and electrician about to depart in Lizzy. They were hoping to buy some part to fix the indicators which, incidentally, had packed up during the previous weekend, and which I had forgotten about in all the excitement. Anyway, rather than have them take Lizzy (and guzzle *my* petrol) I gave them the keys to the car so they might use that to go searching for spares.

Now when I'd gone home to collect the kids and food I found our night guard, Rafael, was there, most upset that on pay day he'd been underpaid by K60 (almost half his wages) and wanted Ziggy to sort it out. So I had brought him with me to the Club.

I explained the situation to Ziggy, who'd been waiting in the bar, also telling him that the mechanics had gone off in his car in search of the spare parts.

"Well, I'll take Rafael along to Rhinestone in the Land Rover," he said, finishing his beer, "which is now fixed apart from the indicator problem."

So off they went.

Fifteen minutes later he was back, saying the Land Rover had died at the traffic lights at the top of the road, so he'd left the night-guard watching over it until the mechanics returned.

When the mechanics drove back they had seen Lizzy at the traffic lights. One had stayed there whilst the other reported to Ziggy, before returning to join his associate.

"Well, I don't have to wait for them, do I?" Ziggy said, finishing off his beer. "I can take Rafael along to the office in the car now."

So off he went. He piled himself and the night-guard into the car, only to find that he couldn't get the car started. So the mechanics had to leave off working on Lizzy and sort out the car instead. Fortunately whatever the problem was with the car, it wasn't major, and Ziggy was soon on his way to Rhinestone.

An hour later, the mechanics drove the Yellowy/Green Goddess into the Club car park, assuring me that it was now working perfectly. I set them up with a couple of Cokes while they waited for Ziggy to give them a lift back to work.

I don't know about vehicle engines, but by the time Ziggy returned to the club at the end of his working day, I was pretty well oiled myself, having spent the best part of three hours at the theatre bar.

With Ziggy and the kids following me in the Peugeot, I drove very carefully home and Lizzy only died when we stopped in front of our gates. Miraculously it started again after only half a dozen attempts and was re-installed back inside our premises.

On Thursday we had further trouble and it was decided that the whole issue would be sorted if a new condenser was fitted. So it was and it worked.

Whilst all this malarkey had been going on, the kids had been behaving remarkably well, so in the afternoon I decided to drive to the Parklands shops and treat them to some chocolate, a rare commodity that I'd heard had recently hit the shelves. Alas, when we arrived we found that the astronomically priced confectionery had already sold out and we had to settle for some sherbet instead.

Back in Tin Lizzy, we exited the car park and had only travelled about ten yards down the road when that familiar shortness of breath appeared beneath my right foot. As I sat there pumping air, another Land Rover, complete with a Zambian Police Sergeant, drew up alongside and, waving his arms, shouted at me to move my vehicle off the highway.

It was all I could do not to shout back to him that I would *love* to move my blasted vehicle. Thankfully he appeared to be on business more important than sorting out traffic problems, and drove off.

Then someone I knew saw my dilemma and pulled up in front of me. Before he could even get out of his car, another policeman came alongside, shouting at *him* not to block the highway. By the time my friend had re-parked his car and come back, some twenty locals had gathered round, waiting to participate in the Zambian national pastime of pushing vehicles. It was all I could do to persuade them that it would be pointless push-starting the Land Rover, but at least they were able to move it to a more police-friendly spot.

This time I left the vehicle under the watchful eye of a cigarette vendor, to whom I paid one *kwacha*, promising him another if everything was in order when I returned later. My friend then drove us round to his nearby house from where I was able to call Ziggy to relate my most recent, and now familiar, plight.

After collecting me from my friend's house, Ziggy drove back to Parklands, intending to use the Peugeot to tow the Land Rover when, naturally, we found that it worked first time and I was able to drive it home.

On Friday morning Ziggy phoned Land Rover in Ndola, wanting to tell them to come and take the bloody useless heap of junk away. Instead he explained our problems and they promised to send someone over that day. Two mechanics arrived at 4:40. Within thirty minutes the main man had sussed out the problem, the timing was all wrong. He sorted it out and took it for a test drive. He returned to our house to have it die on him whilst he was waiting for the gates to be opened.

He looked at it again.

"Ah, *now* I see the problem," He said. "The flood valve in the carburetor is sticking. But don't worry, it'll work itself right with a bit of wear."

Oh, that's alright then, I thought. *As if!*

He hit it a couple of times with the handle of his screwdriver then it started, no problem. After testing it a few times he and his pal left at about 5:50.

"Right, kids," I grinned, "let's go and surprise Daddy at the Cricket Club."

We locked up the house and piled into the car and Benton came out of his house to open the gates for us.

Lizzy, of course, wouldn't start.

"Madam," Benton said, "do you think it might work if you hit that thing which the man kept hitting?"

Anything was worth a try so we opened the bonnet whereupon Benton proceeded to hit 'that thing' with a key. As this proved fruitless I took over and hit it with the end of my key ring and we eventually got it working. Benton was most concerned that I should take something with me to hit 'that thing with' lest it fail again, so I showed him a brick-sized piece of wood that Ziggy had installed in the LR for the purpose of propping up the new jack, which hadn't been quite high enough to reach the jacking point.

Confident now that I could handle the situation, Benton let me out of the gate. As usual I got as far as the end of our road when it died again at the T-junction. I tried to start it normally but eventually got out, armed with my brick-sized piece of hardwood, and proceeded to clonk the carburetor in the appropriate place. That did the trick. Then it stopped again halfway to the Club but this time I was able to re-start it normally. Things were looking up.

The third time it died, despite frantic revving to keep it going, we were at a set of traffic lights on red. I am sure you can imagine the effect it had on the assorted onlookers when a *Mzungu* madam got out of the driver's seat, lifted the bonnet and started hitting the engine with a brick.

"Eish, Madam, I don't think you should be doing that. Perhaps if we push it for the madam…"

Thanking the concerned gentleman for his advice, and offer of help, I crashed the bonnet down, clambered back into the driver's seat, and much to the crowd's astonishment started up and promptly drove off.

When we eventually arrived at the Cricket Club it was not in the triumphant manner I had envisaged. I was a little dishevelled and grubby and Ziggy, of course, was not so enamoured by the thought that we would probably have to repeat similar procedures on the way back.

Just before we arrived, Ziggy had been chatting with a bloke at the bar. He mentioned our 'trouble with a Land Rover' and hit the jackpot. It turned out this chap had spent ten years in the British Army where his sole job was to service Land Rovers. He told Ziggy exactly what the problem was.

Ziggy then persuaded the Rhinestone mechanic and electrician to come and look at it on Sunday and, after explaining what he'd been told would solve the problem, they managed to get the thing working perfectly.

Whoopee!

What's more, Ziggy's army pal was adamant that, once in perfect working order, a Land Rover engine was one of the most reliable. Time would prove that he was right.

* * * * *

Of course that didn't mean that all fun and games with the Land Rover were over. Far from it.

We had just had the pleasure of a long weekend in Zambia, the 6th and

7th being Bank holidays so I was in pretty desperate need of doing some shopping. The company mini-bus had collected the kids for school and Ziggy was on his way out. I decided to leave at the same time, while the gates were open, when I was accosted by Benton.

"Oh Madam," he called "I think I should tell you what Rafael told me this morning."

I waited, intrigued, and so did Ziggy.

"He said that he'd seen rats scuttling about underneath the Land Rover last night, and thought they might have been in the engine."

"Right, I'll be off then," said Ziggy, and he hastily set off in the direction of his car before I had chance to make any response or requests.

The heartless git! All the time we had parked his car in the very same spot, rats had made no appearance on the scene, but now they had to show a keen interest in Lizzy.

I eventually went outside and gingerly raised the bonnet. Although rat-sized droppings could be seen on the battery, everything appeared to be rat-free and quiet. I then opened the door and was horrified to see that not only had the little blighters been in the engine, they had also crapped on my *pink seats*!

I collected the dustpan and brush from the broom cupboard and removed all signs of the offensive turds from the seats as well as all other flat surfaces. I then had the gardener rattle a brush under and around the seats to make sure there was nothing hiding there.

While he was doing that, I banged on the bonnet and wheel arches to discourage any ill-advised rodent from remaining there. Then while still standing outside, I switched on the engine to make absolutely sure nothing wanted to hang around. Satisfied that all was well, I got in and Clement went off to open the gates.

Once settled in, I selected reverse gear though I must admit I had trouble finding it. On the third attempt it engaged and I was about to release the handbrake when I felt what seemed like a thread of cotton, or a fly, settle on my foot. Curious, I casually glanced down when a massive rat *ran across my lap* before disappearing into the dash area on the passenger side.

I screamed, several times, as I frantically tried to get out of my seat, only to find that I couldn't move because I had my seatbelt on. In my panic I forgot I needed to undo the damn thing. After what seemed to be an eternity of fumbling I managed to unbuckle it and half jumped/half fell out of the door before running off towards the fence surrounding Benton's *khaya*.

By this time Clement was racing up the drive, Benton was tearing out of the kitchen, all Benton's kids were screaming in fright at *my* screaming, and every dog in the neighbourhood was barking or howling.

I tell you what, it's the biggest wonder my pretty pink dralon seats weren't now a shade of brown, because I had nearly shat myself.

Oh, I don't know if I can carry on writing this, it's giving me the heebie-jeebies just thinking about it!

Needless to say, it took me a good fifteen minutes to calm down, after which I got Benton and Clement to do a very thorough search of the vehicle for any remaining rodents. Having seen the direction it had gone, though in my panic I was uncertain, I concluded that I couldn't be sure it had actually left the vehicle. There were so many nooks and crannies where something as wily as a rat could lodge itself, most of which we couldn't access to check out.

To say that I was reluctant to get back in and drive the blasted thing was the understatement of the decade. However, after another twenty minutes I realised there was little point in putting it off. I would have to brave 'the elements' and take a chance. Benton clearly found the whole incident pretty funny, but tried not to show it.

"Ah, but Madam," he said "I am sure the rat will have gone now."

"It's all very well for you," I retorted "you're going back into the kitchen. I'm the one who has to get in there and drive the blasted thing!"

He found that even more amusing and lost his battle to control a snigger. But it was no good. I figured that if the thing was still *in situ*, it would probably remain there for goodness knows how long if Lizzy didn't move about. I had to bite the bullet.

Again I started the engine before getting in, then gingerly hoisted myself onto the seat, though I didn't shut the door completely, nor did I put on my seat belt. I slowly released the handbrake and coasted down the drive.

I got as far as the gate, where I needed to put it in gear, then lost my nerve. I put on the brake and jumped out. I was still terrified that a rat would drop down onto my foot as soon as I engaged the clutch. I called Clement to come and bang a stick on (and under) the dashboard until I was happy nothing was still in there. Eventually I climbed back inside, fastened my seatbelt, shut the door and very, very slowly drove off.

I have never had such a nerve-racking drive in all my life. Every time I went round a corner or over a bump, and believe me, there are lots of those on Zambian roads, I had a fear of a rat falling out of the dashboard onto my feet. It was all I could do to concentrate on driving in a straight line, and when a vehicle came towards me I had to make a concerted effort to remain calm, fearing that if a rat appeared then, I might swerve into a head-on collision. By the time I reached town I was quivering like a jelly in an earthquake.

Fortunately there were no more incidents of rats involving Lizzy (or anywhere else) but to be on the safe side I got Ziggy to call in the pest control people and they put poison down in suitable places that were inaccessible to dogs or kids.

With all the other wildlife lurking around in Zambia, I had certainly not anticipated this type of experience. Give me a couple of lions and elephants any day. At least they can't hide in your dashboard!

15

The Treasure Hunt

One day I heard that a small band of members at the Theatre Club were trying to organise a treasure hunt. I had never participated in one so added my name to the list on the posted notice. Anyone who was prepared to be a driver had to tick a box and state the make of their vehicle. I declined that option, not having a clue what might be involved.

Ziggy announced that he had absolutely no intention of getting roped in, but agreed to look after the kids whilst I was off 'doing whatever it is you're going to do'.

On the Saturday afternoon dedicated to this detective work, all interested parties gathered at the Club and at 14:30 the participants were herded into the theatre's Green Room for instructions. Luckily it was a large room!

We were told that each team would consist of one vehicle, with its driver, and four other people. As the folk began clustering into their groups, a loud banging was heard. It was one of the organisers beating a table with his beer bottle.

"Hold it right there, people. You don't start off that easy," said Mighty Mike, leader of the Fearsome Five organising committee. There were a few groans from around the room.

"Every one of you must come to me and draw a slip of paper out of this hat." He produced a top hat and shook it furiously. "Each slip contains one line from a limerick. You must find the people with the other lines for your limerick and that will be your team."

"What?"

"EH?"

"You've gotta be kiddin!"

"No way!"

Moans, groans and comments of varying degrees of vulgarity, could be heard around the room.

"That'll take us *ages*."

"Then you'd better get searching instead of bitching about it, hadn't you?"

Pandemonium. Chaos. Mayhem. None of those words come close to describing what ensued.

"Has anyone got anything which rhymes with Kitty?" called a hopeful Neil standing by the door

About half a dozen women helpfully answered.

"I have."

"I've got two."

"And me!"

"Largest ones over here."

Then Pete chirped up.

"I'm looking for something like a tart."

"Aren't we all," replied several of the male contingency.

"Stop, stop, *stop!*" cried our Leader again. "We'll be here 'til Tuesday at this rate."

He stood on a chair.

"Right, everyone look at me, and if I point to you you're to call out your limerick line. Then whoever thinks they have a line that goes with it, shout it out, then stay together. I'll carry on until you're all in your teams."

"Right," he said, pointing at Steve, "you first."

"Was known to be fond of the gin," read Steve.

After several seconds, "I've got it, I've got it." Joan cried triumphantly. "A budding young actress named Lynn."

A cheer went up, almost drowning out William, reciting "One day she got drunk."

"As the proverbial skunk," yelled Tom

"And the audience said, 'What a sin'," finished off Margaret.

The place was in an uproar. Everyone laughing and cheering and slapping each other on the back as if they had all got it right.

"Calm down, calm down, everybody," hollered Mike, banging his beer bottle again. "If you carry on like this it'll be Thursday, not Tuesday, before we're finished."

The room settled down.

"Pete, you next."

And so it went on, a little more controlled now, and although there were some stumbles, trying to find middles to match beginnings and ends, by the time it came down to the last three teams it was a doddle.

The rest of the limericks went like this:

There was a young lad from Ndola

Tried to woo a young lady named Lola.

But try as he might

He could not get her tight

She would only drink plain Coca Cola.

A lad on the mines known as Andy

Was reputed to love a good brandy

But he stood not a chance

When it came to a dance

Cos the girls thought it made him too randy.

A young lady was looking quite glum
So I bought her a glass of dark rum
The idea was sound
But reality found
That she finished up flat on her bum.

An old friend of mine called Kerry
Had a yearning for medium sherry
When Christmas came round
She could always be found
By the tree, unashamedly merry.

Partaking of three shots of whisky
Was considered to be rather risky,
As one thing was for sure,
If she had any more,
The young lady would end up quite frisky.

There was a young lady called Kitty
Who wasn't renowned to be pretty.
With a vodka and Coke,
And a packet of smokes,
She would sit in her house in the city.

Gill mounted the Speaker's Chair next.

"Attention everyone!" She shouted. "Now I want you all to come and get from me your Treasure Sheet. Your Team Name is the name of the drink in your limerick."

"Read it through to make sure you understand it," she went on, "but don't bother to ask me stupid questions, because you'll only be given stupid answers."

A member from each team fetched a sheet, returning to their group as all then pored over it.

More groans, grumbles and hoots of laughter filled the room as we saw what we had to accomplish on our treasure hunt.

Five minutes later our attention was called for again.

"Right, boys and girls," said Jane, another member of the Fearsome Five, "When I blow this whistle you have exactly 120 minutes to accomplish your tasks. For those of you who can't do maths, (or who work for the mine) that means two hours. We want everyone back here, in this room, with or without all your bits and pieces, with or without a beer in your hand."

"On your marks, get set, *phrrrrip*."

The whistle seemed to have lost its pea, but nonetheless there was a stampede for the door.

Our team consisted of three of my friends, Susan, Lynn and Alan. The fifth member, Geoff, had only recently joined the Nkana Kitwe Art Society and I don't know how he got roped into this shebang but he looked decidedly uneasy about the whole thing.

While other vehicles where loading up and tearing out of the car park, we stood by our transport and discussed strategy. Of all the things we had to collect, I reckoned that, one way or another, we could come up with most of them at my house.

One of the clues for one 'treasure' was the address, written in anagram form, of someone whose signature we had to get. We decided that could be looked at and solved somewhere along the way and would be better left until last, as we figured the other teams would be queuing for it first.

We jumped into Alan's car and after calling at his office, headed for McFrazier Avenue.

Peter was still acting as a day guard at our house during the weekend should we want to go out. Usually he would keep himself occupied with some little jobs he'd find to do around the place in our absence. Knowing that we'd gone to the Club, he was somewhat surprised when I turned up at the gate, and asked me if he should leave now I was back. I told him we weren't here to stay, and that I had a few little 'jobs' he could help me with.

Peter was a smashing guy, very bright and always eager to help, so I gave him an idea of what this was all about. He was not at all fazed by the stupidity of it all, he was, by now, quite used to the Patras family and their loopy friends.

This is what we had to do or find, and how we accomplished it:

• *A hard boiled egg.*

We decided to trust our newcomer, Geoff, with this so I pointed him in the direction of the kitchen.

• *A green feather.*

By a stroke of luck I'd brought a selection of feathers back from the UK with me, for the Club wardrobe.

• *A live frog*

This is where Peter came in. I asked him to search around the garden for a frog, the biggest he could find. It wasn't easy as there weren't many around at that time of year, the dry season.

- *A child's catapult.*

Which I got Peter to make after he'd caught the frog.

- *A strapless bra.*

I gave an old bra of mine to Geoff to cut the straps off.

- *A pin-up photograph.*

We tore out the centrefold from a girly magazine Ziggy had brought from the UK, and boy was it a 'hot' one.

- *The sound of a dog barking, on tape.*

This is why we had gone to Alan's office. He collected a spool of telex tape and we wrote the words *WOOF WOOF WOOF*, on it.

- *A sweet potato.*

I didn't have any so we got an ordinary one, wiped it with a damp cloth and shook it around in a plastic bag containing icing sugar. (We earned more points for this than others who had taken a real sweet potato!)

- *A limerick about beer recorded on tape.*

It was a good job Alan had brought along a full roll of telex tape. Here's how the beer limerick went:

What is hoppy and brings us good cheer?
Not a froggy, of that I am clear!
It is brown, black or tan,
And might come in a can.
It's undoubtedly wonderful beer!

- *A photograph of a member of the team as a baby (under 1 year).*

Fortunately I had one.

- *A cane penny whistle.*

We thought of getting Peter to make us one, but he was too busy chasing frogs around the garden and trying to make a catapult. Instead we found a piece of cane in the garden and stuck a one penny coin to it with Sellotape, then Geoff would whistle a tune when he presented it to the judges.

- *An Instant Whip.*

That was too easy. As virtually every household had a packet of that desert in their cupboards (it being about the only convenience pudding available in Kitwe) we decided to be different. One of us would wear a belt, which would be quickly removed in front of the judges and used to 'whip' the nearest convenient person.

- *Dress up.*

Three members of the team had to appear dressed as the following:

In a bathing costume
In sporting gear
As a Red Indian.

Sue had the privilege of that. She wore a T-shirt of mine which had long tassels, braided her long hair, did her best at war-paint with my make-up, and we tied ribbons onto our axe for her to brandish.

Alan offered to wear my one and only swimsuit, which he had to wear back to front otherwise it would never have covered the necessary bits. The fact that it showed most of his ass was neither here nor there. The low back, now at the front, also showed off his hairy chest a treat.

I then donned my slinky black baby-doll nightie and had one of the girls write, in big letters, "I'm A Sport" in black eyeliner on my right thigh and "I'm Game" on the left one.

With this ensemble we couldn't fail!

We gathered up all our treasure and headed out to the car. Poor Peter nearly died laughing when he saw us all, as he handed over the frog (in a Tuppaware box I'd given him) and his finely crafted catapult, before letting us out the gate.

Our final mission was to collect that signature, but of whom we had no idea. When we arrived at the unscrambled address we realised it must be someone pretty loaded as it was a very grand house.

We were obviously expected because as we pulled up outside the electronic gates they slowly swung open to let us onto the property. As he was not wearing anything outlandish, we had nominated Geoff to collect the signature but as he was about to get out of the car the front door opened and a very imposing figure walked out. Geoff made a sort of strangled noise and said there no way was he going to fetch it. The figure in question happened to be one of the head honchos at ZCCM, where Geoff had just started work.

As everyone else was holding onto various things, Alan got out from the driver seat and walked up to him. The poor bloke's eyes went wide as saucers when he saw Alan in my swimsuit, and involuntarily took a step backwards.

"Good afternoon, Sir," Alan greeted him, as if his attire was quite normal. "I understand you've been expecting us, would you mind…"

Before providing his signature, the Director quickly recovered his composure and replaced his expression of incredulity with a broad grin.

"Well, I was expecting another group of people looking for my signature, but I wasn't quite expecting … this!" and waved expansively at Alan's somewhat vulgar and ill-fitting attire.

"Yes, sorry Sir. Not my normal choice, but you know what that theatrical lot are like at NKAS," Alan said, "got no shame."

"What else have you got hidden in there?" asked the director, nodding at the car.

Alan shouted for us all to come out. As we paraded before him, prancing in keeping with our newly found characters, the poor man erupted into laughter. As he laughed and spluttered I wasn't sure if he was about to choke to death or have a heart attack.

"But I thought there were five in each team," he said, when he recovered, "where's the other one?"

"Oh, he's in the car looking after the frog … and he's very shy."

"Well, he's clearly on his own with that one," laughed the honcho. "Well, here's your signature, and with all the effort you've put in, I hope you guys win."

We got back to the Club with time to spare. Before going inside, Allen donned a blanket from the boot of his car to hide his skimpy attire, then we sent Geoff and Lynn to the bar to get us a round of drinks. The doors to the Green Room had been firmly closed so we all hung around in the Copper Bar, an extension of the theatre's main bar, which could be closed off when necessary. (As you might imagine, it got its name from the bar counter which was overlaid with beaten copper.)

At precisely 17:30 Gill ceremoniously drew back the Green Room doors and stood waiting for silence before she would deliver her diatribe.

"Well, I'm pleased to see that you all made it back in one piece and without being arrested," she began. "We would like to see everyone in the Green Room except the team members who got dressed up."

The Fearsome Five organisers now sat behind two suitably adorned trestle tables on a mini stage.

Once all appropriate folk were inside they asked for the Red Indians to come in.

They paraded before the Judges quietly, until Lynn started doing a war dance, shaming the others into joining in. The Judges made notes on the pads in front of them then called for the Sports People.

In went a cricketer, rugby player, tennis pro, a horse rider (without the horse), a couple of golfers and then came me, accompanied by wolf whistles and cat-calls from the attending audience.

Then came the Bathing Beauties. What an assortment that presented, with old-fashioned bloomers and frills of the late 1800's and of course the men's knee length striped garb, there were also snorkels and flippers in evidence.

But when Alan walked in baring his extremely hairy chest and a lot of other stuff which shouldn't have been bared but was still difficult to fully conceal in a ladies swimsuit, the whole place went into hysterics.

When everyone had eventually calmed down the judges pointed to the person in each category who had gained the most points. We took all three! We were certainly off to a good start.

Once team members were reunited, all the individual treasures were called up. The amount of effort and imagination which had gone into many of the items placed before the judges was far greater than anyone expected. Their presentation (and in some cases, explanations) took considerable time, but no-one was clock watching.

The barmen from the main bar, being deprived of most of their customers, provided a constant waiter service into the Green Room.

We eventually came to the last item to be called. The frog.

Apart from a couple of teams who had given up their search for anything remotely frog-like, each team presented some form of frog – toy, ornament or pictures. I made sure I went last.

Holding my Tuppaware container I swanned up to the stage in my slinky black nightie, and as I gained and maintained sweeping eye contact with each of the Fearsome Five, carefully removed the lid, then quickly tipped out the frog onto the middle of the judges' table.

Shrieks and squeals burst forth from the stage, as chairs got knocked over and our esteemed judges fell over each other in their haste to avoid being leapt on by the now very pissed off, none too small frog, who hopped wildly around the table obviously trying to get away from these loud foreign noises.

Of course, the Green Room had exploded with howls of laughter, there were people holding onto each other for support or bent double clutching stomachs, now aching from so much laughing. Two women beat a hasty retreat to the Ladies' room, clearly on the point of wetting themselves.

Some kind gentleman managed to track down froggy and carried the poor creature out to the car park, leaving him on a boundary by a ditch. I would have preferred to return him to his home in our garden but it wouldn't have been fair to keep him boxed until we went home, which looked like it might be considerably later.

At length things returned to some sense of normality and the slightly dishevelled judges settled back in their seats.

Using a beer bottle once more as a gavel, Mike gained the attention of the room.

"Ladies and Gentlemen, and several we're not sure about," he began, "first of all, I and my fellow adjudicators here," he glanced left and right to his buddies, "would like to thank you all most sincerely for participating so enthusiastically in the NKAS Treasure Hunt. I know I speak for all five of us when I say that we haven't been so wondrously entertained off-stage in decades."

At which all five judges carefully (this time) stood up and applauded the players. In true theatrical style, the majority of us bowed or curtseyed formally in acknowledgment.

"It only remains for me now to announce the winners. Whilst we recognise the incredibly high standard of all the entries here, the total votes counted for this entire escapade leave no doubt at all that the winners, by far, are the *Whisky* team."

"Yeah!"

"Congratulations!"

"Definite winners!"

"Without a doubt!"

"Bravo!"

After we had got over the shock, because there really had been some splendid entries there, we walked up onto the stage to collect our prize, an enormous bottle of wine, for the drinking of.

And was it worth it?

Hell, yes. What a day, and night, we had.

16
A Change of Direction

One day we were chatting to Glyn Jones.

"Who is he?" I hear you ask.

A couple of weeks after our arrival in Kitwe, back in 1980, we were looking for somewhere to celebrate our 6th wedding anniversary. Our special day fell on a Monday. This was precisely when all the eating establishments in Kitwe (apart from the hotel) had the day off. We knew of the existence of the Little Theatre because we had been there the weekend before to watch a film about elephant poaching. We decided to try our luck there, only to discover it was a 'members only' establishment.

Glyn was the guy who had kindly signed us in as his guest that night, introducing us to some of the members and explaining what the place was all about. The rest, as the saying goes, is history.

Now Glyn asked us if, instead of spending the majority of our weekends at the Club, we would be interested in getting together with a gang of mutual friends to visit a few places of interest on a Sunday. We thought it sounded like a cracking idea so the ball rolled, initially in the direction of the Cricket Club, where we would all meet up before trekking off into the bush.

Before we go any further perhaps I should explain about 'the bush'. In Africa we do not refer to it as 'the jungle', despite there being lots of lions around purporting to be the kings of it. In fact the origin of the word 'jungle' referred to dry uncultivated land. An Anglo-Indian interpretation of the word later conjured up an image of a dense, semi-humid forest of tangled thicket, long creepers and semi-naked men swinging from tree to tree. The majority of sub-Saharan Africa is nothing like that.

This is probably why those living in Africa prefer to denote the vast undeveloped land, with or without wild animals, as 'the bush'. It can have open expanses of grassland (savannah) or be more mixed in its vegetation, with trees and bushes of assorted shapes and sizes, and hellishly long grass (elephant grass). The density of this mix varies from region to region.

Anyway, where was I?

Oh yes, rolling into the Cricket Club.

Depending on what else was happening in Kitwe on any given weekend, there could be anything from three to half a dozen vehicles participating in the Sunday adventures. Four vehicles went on the first trip to the 17-mile Dambo, so named because it is a dam 17 miles from Kitwe. We understood that there were picnic areas at a location which we knew formed part of a bird sanctuary. We found a nice picnic spot with *rondavels* (large, round, thatched shades) and *braai* facilities. What we didn't see were any birds.

Maybe they'd heard we were coming and flew off somewhere quieter.

Another weekend a crowd of five sets of wheels went to Mufulira Rapids, about half an hour's drive away, on the nearby Kafue River. This being a popular spot, the access was pretty good.

There was a huge flat rock overlooking the rapids where we parked our cars in a semi-circle before setting up our picnic area with rugs, chairs, picnic tables, unloaded cool-boxes, etc. We noticed quite a large crowd of Indians wandering around down by the edge of the rapids. They must have parked their cars behind some bushes somewhere else since we hadn't seen any sign of them when we first arrived.

As we sat back with our drinks and chatted amongst ourselves, the Indian people returned from the river. Instead of walking a further 20 yards to avoid us, they walked right through the middle of our party, between tables, chairs and people holding conversations.

Some of them even stood around looking at us, as if we were part of the scenery. We sat there, mouths agape, looking back and forth at each other with *what the* expressions on our faces. Fortunately at some silent, unseen signal they all moved off and disappeared to heaven knew where. It was quite a surreal experience.

Whilst the riverine area was very pleasant to sit for the afternoon, it wasn't suitable for bathing as the water was very fast flowing over the series of rocky waterfalls and, once it became more sedate downstream there was the ever present threat of crocodiles.

Our next incursion into the bush was a little more adventurous. We went *bundu* bashing.

When you fly over certain parts of Zambia you can clearly see what looks like interminable, wide roads stretching below. They are, in fact, the clear-ways called way-leaves, repair and maintenance thoroughfares for the main power cables and pylons marching their way across the country. One of our 'gang', Vince, worked for CPC (the Copperbelt Power Company) and he had been told about a likely picnic spot beside a small lake, or dam, along the route of the power lines, several miles outside Kitwe. Being the intrepid explorers that we were, we decided we should check it out.

Vince said that, whilst it could be reached by the CPC access road, which ran beneath the cables, the road was 'likely to be a bit rough'. We should only take bush vehicles on this expedition. Of course we were in a key position here with Lizzy, as were Paul and Jane who had a Range Rover and Jenny and John who had the Toyota version, a Land Cruiser. The Land Cruiser, being open-backed, could carry a small boat, so John arranged to borrow one from a friend, complete with an outboard motor.

We arranged that all those who wanted to go, should meet up at the Cricket Club at 11:00 where distribution of bodies and *katundu* would be made from cars into the 4 by 4s.

On the morning of our trek, Ziggy had been into work and only returned at 11:00 so there was a mad rush to load all our stuff into Lizzy. We arrived at the Cricket Club to be told that John had phoned to say he and Jenny were 'running a little late, collecting the boat'. When Paul and Jane pitched up in their Range Rover, we thought we should sit down to discuss who was going to travel with whom. It suddenly occurred to me that I didn't see Ziggy pack our *braai* box. A quick question confirmed this so we hoped that others had remembered theirs. We found the 'car people' in the bar and, over a beer, we discovered that between us we had two *braais* to feed twelve adults and a herd of kids. John and Jenny eventually arrived and of course needed to get suitably refreshed (with a beer) before departure.

As we poured into the car park to load up, Paul reckoned it was hardly worth moving now and suggested we set up shop on the edge of the cricket pitch instead. He was beaten ferociously from several quarters before we all crammed, and I mean crammed, into the vehicles.

Into John's went him and Jenny and all the bags, with boxes and *braais* wedged in with the boat. Into Paul's went him and Jane and their baby, Pete and Karen and their baby, and John Brandrick who was flying solo as his wife, Joan, was currently in the UK. In ours there was me driving, Ziggy, Glyn, Vince and Sandra, their two kids, John and Jenny's two kids and of course, our three kids. With Vince navigating, we set off. Paul had left while we were still loading up as he needed to get beers on the way. John also had to stop for beers and petrol and followed us out.

"Who's got the bottle opener?" someone piped up five minutes after we set off.

"More to the point," somebody else asked, "where are the beers?"

We realised with dismay that all our beers were in the back of John's wagon.

We ambled up the dual carriageway for some time before turning into the road leading to Kamfinsa Prison. We'd almost reached there when someone remarked they didn't recall passing Paul along the way. Spotting a roadside tavern, it seemed like the perfect place to stop and wait.

It was a typical Zambian tavern with loud, semi-tuneless, twangy guitar music blaring out from the bar. Unfortunately for the kids, the bar did not sell any soft drinks. The bonus was that the beers were ice cold. The adults were about to start on a second round when Paul turned up and joined in the exercise.

We had just got the third round in when John and Jenny arrived. Apparently the service station they called at, about half way along, turned out to be closed, so they had to drive all the way back to Kitwe to fill up.

Goodness knows what time we left that bar but only a mile further down the road we found the power lines. Vince called a halt.

"Turn right here," he said.

"Onto what?" I asked.

When he pointed it out, I could barely make out the CPC maintenance track.

"Are you serious?"

It wasn't the track I was worried about, it was the six feet by three feet deep *donga* (storm-water drainage ditch) that ran parallel to the road that bothered me.

To avoid getting wedged in I had to take it at an angle and Lizzy leaned heavily over to the right as I drove down. We rocked a bit, as the front end went up the opposite bank, before the rear wheels hit the bottom, then leaned even further over to the left as I slowly climbed out. I thought the thing was going to tip over. Of course, Lizzy could manage much more than that piddling little ditch, but this was my first attempt at 'rough' driving and it was very unnerving. Naturally for the old hands behind me it was a doddle.

We drove on down the maintenance track, which was fairly passable as tracks went. As far as we knew there weren't any elephants in this area but the track was bordered by the elephant grass customarily found in the bush. After about half a mile we reached the 'picnic area'. It wasn't quite what we had envisaged and certainly not typical of those provided by municipalities.

To prepare for our visit, Vince had sent one of his workers during the week to clear the area of the long grass with a slasher. Yes, yes, I know, that does need clarification.

A 'slasher' is a Zambian lawn mower. Actually, it is a gardening tool which consists of a length of flat metal about an inch-and-a-half wide and three feet long, attached to a wooden grip at one end and six inches of the other bent up at a 45° angle with both edges honed sharp. The slasher was swung back and forth slicing through the grass just above ground level.

The trouble was that the worker, on this occasion, was either exceedingly tall or had a very short slasher. He left about nine inches of 'stubble' which was now very dry and spiky. As we piled out of the wagons the most enthusiasm we could muster was to say that at least it was different. Fortunately John saved the day by magically producing a large tarpaulin which we spread on the ground and stomped on to flatten the stubble beneath.

Whilst we'd been refreshing ourselves at the Zambian tavern, we had established that not one person had remembered to bring charcoal. Fortunately, as we were about to send John back into Kitwe once again to buy some, a little man came trundling along the road on a bicycle loaded with an enormous sack of charcoal. We told him we'd like to buy it but it was so big we couldn't fit it in any of the vehicles. We asked him to follow us to our destination and the poor soul had to pedal it all the way down to the dam. It didn't seem to bother him, not with the promise of a good sale to some crazy English people at the end of his journey.

The afternoon then progressed into a very enjoyable affair. We took turns to use Vince's tiny *braai* and Paul's plough disc. A plough disc is a round, slightly dished, hefty piece of metal about 18 inches across which sits on a three-legged stand, under which you light your charcoal. It has the added bonus of being able to fry up potatoes, onions and tomatoes as well as the meat. Yummy.

Then followed the silliness. The boat had already been launched and tested a few times so we decided to have races. Since there was only one boat we had to race against the clock. We split into teams. Ziggy was the official time-keeper and two ladies abstained so there were three teams of two men and one team of three ladies.

Each team began at the starting block, in this case a rock, and we drew straws (pieces of lopped grass) to see who would go first. Carrying a bottle of beer, we had to race down to the water's edge, leap in the boat, start the motor then charge across the dam, do a figure of eight around a small island and an even smaller clump of reeds then back to the shore, tie up the boat then run back to the starting rock. The clock stopped when the empty (consumed) beer bottle was slammed down on a table next to the rock.

As it happened the ladies team didn't do too well as the engine cut out when we were between the island and the clump of reeds and it took us five and a half minutes to restart it. And the rotten time-marshal wouldn't give us time off, the miserable so-and-so. But it was so much fun and I have no idea who the winners were.

Suffice it to say that it turned into a jolly good day out. We packed up and left (leaving nothing behind except the flattened grass) before it got dark. Believe me you don't want to still be sitting around at dusk because it gets dark very quickly in Zambia.

We returned to the Cricket Club, so that the assorted passengers could transfer into their own cars, but were compelled to go in for a drink in order to discuss our next trip. It was decided to go to a place called Rodwins, about twelve kilometres from Kitwe, where it too had a lake with designated picnic areas and boats which one could hire. *And* it had proper toilets! Much gentler on the backside (for the ladies) than the spiky elephant grass behind a bush.

But it couldn't have been as much fun as our CPC picnic because I didn't write home about it.

* * * * *

As the weeks rolled along, I was once more embroiled in things theatrical. Paul McDermott was putting on another production and, as was becoming the norm, wanted me to do the costumes. This one was Shakespeare's *Hamlet.*

Like the first play I had worked on for him in 1981 (*The Crucible*), the colour scheme was chiefly black and white. On that basis I thought there wouldn't be that much work involved for me. Of course I was way off the mark. Whilst the colours (or lack thereof) might have been similar, the period was such that the style of clothing was totally different. So it was back to the drawing board or, to be more precise, the sewing machine.

I also had a walk-on part in this one too, as a nun. I accompanied Ophelia on-stage at a point not long before she topped herself. Guess I couldn't have been much of a nursemaid.

We nearly wreaked total havoc on the final night. Someone had told us a joke before we went on stage which involved a funny facial expression. At a point when Marion, who played the part of Ophelia, had her back to the audience, she made a similar face at me. It was so unexpected I really battled not to laugh. As I tried to keep my face straight my eyes got wider and my lips tightened and this set Ophelia off. As she screwed up her face to try to control herself, the rest of the cast thought she was putting on a particularly moving performance. I, too, was commended for having real tears rolling down my cheeks.

Neither of us got an award for our performances, though Marion was praised by one of the local newspaper critics. Oh, and I won the annual award for Best Costumes, again.

* * * * *

As I mentioned earlier, membership of the Nkana Kitwe Art Society was conditional on the members physically contributing to the operation of the theatre, be it on stage, backstage or in any other capacity in which the theatre might benefit. This kept out the people who wanted to use it solely as a tavern.

Unfortunately one of the things which had attracted us to that club in the first place, the pool, was the cause of the change in the theatre as we knew it.

It was decided in the winter of '83 that the theatre's pool should be repainted. Pools in Zambia were not tiled and needed to be painted to protect the structure. A special chlorinated rubber paint was used for the job. The Club pool was pretty big, about twenty yards long by eight wide, and consisted of two ten by eight areas overlapped at the corner. One area was the shallow end which then stepped down to the other, deeper, end.

As the Club didn't have sufficient funds to have it painted professionally, it had to be done by members. A few of our Zambian members proposed their friends, who could help paint the pool, and so earn their membership. They in turn proposed and seconded more friends, and before we knew it the Club membership had doubled. And because very few people knew who was who, since they were coming and going at different times, we weren't certain who had legitimately helped and who had not.

What we did know was that, when the painting of the pool had been completed, a whole new crowd of members, without the slightest interest in the theatre, were using the Club solely as a drinking hall.

I recall one evening when we were frantically working on stage and in the final throes of rehearsals for one production. We were reaching a point where we could stop for a break and I went off to the bar to fetch everyone's drinks. Two barmen were on duty on this particular night and I couldn't attract the attention of either of them. Both were busy serving a particularly loud group of drinkers who couldn't decide what they all wanted. The situation was not helped by the barmen laughing and joking along with them.

Time was very tight for us in this rehearsal and, exasperated, I went behind the bar and helped myself to beers. That soon got the barmen's attention.

Despite their protests I continued to organise my drinks order and left a note of everything I had taken, together with a promise to return and pay when they weren't so busy (which of course I did, when we had finished on stage). A couple of days later I was tackled by the Committee member in charge of the bar.

"What the hell did you think you were doing, helping yourself behind the bar?"

"I needed service, and I clearly wasn't going to get any before it was time to resume rehearsals."

"Well, you can't just go helping yourself."

"Then you had better sort out your bar staff, Mr Manager, and tell them where their priorities lie. Because, if those working on stage, or back stage, are unable to get timely refreshments, the Club could soon find itself very short of working and acting members!"

"Fair point. I'll have a word with the staff," he conceded, "but please don't do it again."

Alas, 'his word with the staff' really didn't seem to do much good, and as far as many of us were concerned the Theatre Club was losing its attraction as a place to spend so many of our social hours.

17

McFrazier to Mwande

In an effort to be able to spend more time at home, I was still keeping my eyes and ears open for a house with a pool. I heard that an expat family I knew of were moving to South Africa and we considered exchanging houses as theirs had a pool.

Ziggy had left me to do the house hunting and refused to view it, saying he'd seen it once before when he dropped Brad off there for a party. He had been invited in for a beer, and from what he remembered, it was okay.

When I went to see it I found the inside was rather dark and the *khaya* area would need to be walled off from the pool area for privacy. Although it had a separate bathroom from shower-room, there was only a wash basin in one of them, which would get very crowded with five of us cleaning our teeth at the same time in the morning. It also needed a few repairs done. But it *did* have a pool.

We were only a few days away from getting Rhinestone to sign a lease agreement and I had already made curtains because the old ones from Frazer Crescent wouldn't fit. I sent our gardener round there to do a bit of clearing up and when, after lunch, I said I would be going to check how he was doing, Ziggy accompanied me.

He walked through with me whilst I explained to him the repairs which were required and which up to now he had only seen written down. He promptly announced that he did not like the house.

"It's too dark, the garden is too small and too much work needs doing to it, most of which we'll have to pay for I suspect. So I don't want to live here."

I could have murdered him.

"You might have come and seen it and made that decision *before* I'd spent K996 on new curtains!" I fumed.

He then had the cheek to say that Ray Milton's house in Mwande had become vacant and that we'd probably be better moving there. 'Ray Milton's house' was none other than the one we were offered back in January, when Ziggy first took over his new position. Except that Ray Milton had managed to get most of the work done that Rhinestone had refused to do for us! And he was at a much lower job level than Ziggy. Of course, his advantage had been that he crept so far up the ass of the Managing Director that he could almost have cleaned his (the MD's) teeth from the inside!

Dear All,

OK folks, we actually made it. The new house. The gentle throbbing of the pool pump is music to my ears. But what a mission it was getting here.

After I last wrote to you we started packing. We filled a huge trunk with all the books and things off the wall unit, only to find that we couldn't lift it and had to start all over again, putting them into small cardboard boxes instead.

Trundling backwards and forwards in Lizzy, by the Friday night I had the majority of stuff round at Mwande leaving only the large furniture, beds, bedding and our clothes to be shifted. Or so I thought. I had forgotten about the carpets, garden furniture, and the contents of the food store cupboards, not to mention the fridges and freezers.

By the Sunday night we and all our possessions were firmly if haphazardly stashed in our new abode. Then we realised that our problems had only just begun. The kitchen is only half the size of our previous one with commensurately fewer cupboards, and the only other storage in the house is the wardrobes in the bedrooms, with the two boys having to share one. Where on earth are we going to put everything? The only saving grace is that the passageway to the bedrooms is quite wide, so at least we can stack the unpacked boxes there.

Only now do I truly appreciate how appropriately we had named the Big House.

So it was that I now fumbled around in cupboards and trawled through countless boxes during the following months. I rued the day I had insisted on leaving the Big House. The simple act of baking a cake became a marathon search for special baking items, decorations and pans, because it was necessary to utilise what little cupboard space I had in the kitchen for regularly used equipment and commodities. But when I heard the constant squeals of delight and laughter, from the kids having fun outside in the pool, I realised that my discomforts were outweighed by the amount of joy this move had brought.

Whilst Rhinestone might have done some repairs and improvements to the Mwandi Crescent house for the ass-creeper, in some cases this hadn't made much of a difference. They might well have replaced the crabby carpet tiles which had adorned the floors, but they had not been able to completely eradicate the stink of eau de cat, courtesy of the initial householder's pet.

If the house was locked up for any lengthy period of time, for example when we went out for a full day and evening at a weekend, we locked all the doors and windows. This had to be done for security. When we returned we were smacked in the face with the stench of tom-cat pee. All doors and windows were immediately opened but, by the time that was done, you already felt like you'd bathed in the stuff. It makes me nauseous just writing about it.

Another issue which required attention was the swimming pool. It had recently been resurfaced but hadn't yet been painted. It is very important that pools are painted, as the concrete surface eventually corrodes because of the chemicals (chlorine and hydrochloric acid) used to maintain the water fit for bathing. The exiting employee had informed us that, should we want it painted, to get in touch with Penguin Pools who had already been paid for the job and were obliged to complete it.

When Ziggy got around to phoning them they said they were very busy at that time. Ziggy said that if they provided the paint we would get it painted ourselves, by a little company called Robinsons who came around twice a week to clean the pool. Penguin happily agreed to this, so the following week I was to collect the paint.

The woman Ziggy spoke to wasn't there, and the woman who was there, Tina, didn't know anything about it. She said she would 'make enquiries' and that I should phone her at 11 o'clock on Tuesday.

A man answered the phone when I called and said that Tina was off sick and could he help. I had to explain the whole thing again to him, emphasising that I was going to be holding a kids party soon and that I needed it finished before then. After making some enquiries he called me back to say the paint was being collected from Vitretex (the paint manufacturing company) and that it would be ready for my collection from him within half an hour.

When I arrived I was given, after some confusion, five 5-litre tins of white paint. But I didn't want white, I wanted blue. The woman I had spoken to the very first time was now in attendance and chirped up.

"We always paint our pools white. I think it looks much nicer."

I remarked that I had seen both white and blue painted pools and I thought that the blue ones looked better. But as they only had white paint, I grudgingly accepted it. I consulted John, the bloke I'd spoken to on the phone.

"How many coats do I apply?"

"Two. And as the paint is pretty thick you should thin down the first coat."

"Thin it with what?" I asked

"With water," he said.

This is blooming funny pool paint that you thin down with water, I thought to myself. *Like, how is it supposed to stay on once you put water in the pool?*

I had vivid recollections of some peoples' pools which had been painted with some vague substance which came off on your feet, knees, elbows and backside whenever you used their pools. It didn't take much to put two and two together and realise that I had probably been given some of that paint. Suffice it to say that I was not happy. However, I left the premises of Penguin Pools complete with five tins of paint, each of which had a hand-written label stating *Acrylic Swimming Pool Paint*.

When I arrived home I was rather surprised to see the outside ditch full of water. I wasn't aware it had been raining, and even with all my distractions I was sure I would have noticed *that*. As I drove inside I was horrified to find four workers standing around our pool, watching the water drain out. It was already half empty. I could have wept.

"What the devil do you think you're doing?" I cried.

"Agh, Madam, we are emptying your pool for you," he said with a big grin.

"But I didn't want it emptying today. I asked for it to be emptied on Friday."

"Agh but Madam, we are very quick," said another grin-bearer, "and we could do it for you today."

I gave up.

As we were going out over the weekend, I had asked them to empty it on the Friday ready for being painted on the Monday. Today was only Tuesday, and with temperatures at the stinking-hot level it was real swimming weather. Apparently not for us!

After half an hour I had calmed down sufficiently to phone Vitretex. I knew that paint companies had no exchange policies so when a man named Fred answered I explained my problems. I had been given some of his company's paint that I suspected was unsuitable, as well as being the wrong colour. He genuinely sympathised and actually said he was disgusted that someone at Penguin Pools had given me the paint in question. He confirmed that it was normal household matt paint for *internal* use, not even top quality external stuff. Anyway, he said, pools should always be painted with chlorinated rubber paint.

Thankfully he agreed to change it for me and said that Penguin Pools would be charged the difference in price. We then went into a lengthy discussion on what shade of blue would be best when, out of the blue (no pun intended) he asked which company my husband worked for.

"Rhinestone Mechanical," I said.

"What's his name then?"

"Ziggy Patras"

"Well I'll be damned," he said, "I was only talking to him this morning. I'm the Chairman of the Kitwe SPCA and Ziggy phoned me to see if we wanted to take out a Gala booking for the Old Time Music Hall (OTMH) at the Little Theatre this year."

He went on to say that he was meeting Ziggy the following day in regard to the Gala. From that point on, if it was possible, he was even more helpful. I told him I would be there too, being involved with the wardrobe. He said he had recently become a member of the theatre and was in the chorus of the OTMH. He suggested we take the paints there the next day and do a swap.

The Robinson company duly started painting our pool on the Monday morning, and after three coats had been applied, as per Fred's recommendation, they completed it by Tuesday night (paint dried *very* quickly in Zambia). Even so, we couldn't start refilling the pool until Thursday night. This promised to be quite a lengthy process, which turned out to be a bonus.

The kids had a whale of a time during the filling process. The bottom of the pool, being covered in bright, shiny paint, was ideal for sliding on.

Starting at the shallow end, where the drizzling hosepipe lay, the kids took a short run down then skidded along into the water. Left to them I think they would have preferred the pool to be partially empty on a permanent basis.

By the time it was full we were only six days away from Brad's birthday party. It was then that the joys of being a pool custodian became apparent. As we gazed upon this beautifully painted pool, we could not help noticing that its contents resembled *pea-green soup*. We knew, around this time of year, the quality of the municipal water wasn't brilliant, but now possessed the indisputable proof of why one should always boil the tap-water before drinking it. We also knew we needed to take some pretty drastic action to transform this replication of an open-topped septic tank into something more inviting to swim in.

On Monday morning Ziggy phoned Robinsons and asked them to grab their chemicals and come and work miracles, only to be told that the previous Friday Rhinestone had cancelled the company contract with Robinsons, saying that in future all pools would become the responsibility of Rhinestone Civil Maintenance squad. We found this news rather disturbing as in the past the Maintenance squad had wanted nothing to do with Rhinestone's Mechanical division. Probably, we thought, because those in the Mechanical division knew a bit more about what that squad should be doing than *they* did themselves.

But Ziggy managed to work wonders and the squad appeared the next day, looked at the pool, did very little, then disappeared. They came again on the Thursday and, seeing nothing much had improved, declared that they couldn't do much as the pool filter obviously wasn't working properly.

On the day of Brad's party we endeavoured to convince our guests that the swimming facility, which resembled undiluted Roses Lime Cordial, was in fact fit to swim in. The vast amount of chemicals that had been hurled in had the possible drawback of turning all the blonde-haired kids into green-haired kids and the Zambian kids into albinos.

In the event none of the above transpired (you'll be relieved to hear) and the kids didn't give a fig what colour the water was. Brad had a super seventh birthday.

18

Fun on Stage

Of all the productions put on by NKAS, the Old Time Music Hall was one of my favourites. The Kitwe theatre-going public loved it, although we did have a few nights with some empty seats. I reckon this was due to the fact that so many of the Kitwe expats were actually participating in the production.

It usually took place in October and ran for two weekends. There were many regular performers, such as Nellie Cornelious singing *I was Only a Bird in a Gilded Cage* with her amazing birdcage prop, and the Barbershop Quartet, which invariably had five or six members and who never failed to entertain us with their melodic harmonies. But my personal regular favourite was the first act.

The show always opened with the *Cancan*. What a line-up of ladies they were. Never being able to do straight, never mind high, kicks myself, I was always in awe of those girls. Their shapely legs were adorned with black fishnet stockings. Each of the bodices of their black burlesque dresses was trimmed in a bright colour – red, green, yellow, light blue, dark blue, pink or purple, with layers and layers of matching frills under the skirt, and they wore similarly adorned frilly panties to maintain their modesty.

At eight o'clock the auditorium doors were closed. With all lights fully dimmed, the audience would sit in silent anticipation. Then the first six, short sharp bars of Offenbach's *Cancan* began. As the music gathered pace there would be an uproar as the stage lit up and unleashed the ladies in all their splendour.

With knee-bends and wiggles and shoulder-high kicks they were a sight to behold. Their lines moved across and around the stage with amazing symmetry. For such an energetic dance routine, the precision with which it was performed was incredible. Some would do cartwheels across the stage to the squeals and whoops of the others and none of the dancers were ever seen standing still. It culminated in splits and frills and saucily presented bottoms, and a standing ovation with cheers and hoots from the thrilled audience. It would be some time before the extremely verbose Master of Ceremonies, our friend, Gordon Ritchie, was able to calm everyone down so that he could get a plethora of words in.

Each act which followed was individually produced. The whole show would encompass dozens of NKAS members, some of whom would only be seen at this time of year. Stalwarts also joined in, often in positions totally alien to their norm.

The last OTMH that I was involved with is the one I recall most, first because it was the last, and second because I actually participated on stage, three times.

Since buying our video equipment I had managed to get several tapes of British television productions, mostly consisting of comedy stuff, sent out from the UK. There was a show called *Russ Abbot's Madhouse* at the beginning of the '80s which had some hilarious skits, which I had shared with some of my Club friends, and which some tried to emulate. And of course there were Monty Python classics which simply had to be included. One of these was the Cheese Shop sketch which only required two actors, the sales person behind the counter and the optimistic customer.

One of NKAS's top actors, Peter Heath, played the part of the customer. Amongst others, Peter had held major roles in the three huge plays I had organised costumes for, *The Crucible*, *Mary Stuart* and *Hamlet*, and he had received awards for all his performances.

Unfortunately for him, I was cast as the sales person. The poor soul never really stood a chance because I must hang my head in shame and confess that I totally fluffed one of my performances.

I was always pretty lousy at remembering lines. On this one occasion I missed out a response and it totally screwed up some of the best lines. Peter was, quite rightly, absolutely furious with me as we melted offstage when the lights dimmed at the end of the skit.

"You missed out the response to camembert! How could you miss out the response to camembert? It is one of the single most famous lines in the sketch. I don't care how (censored) runny it is, you missed out the camembert!"

"Sorry, Peter."

"Even the cat didn't get to eat it!"

He stormed off. If you haven't seen that Monty Python sketch, do yourself a favour and YouTube it. You'll see what I mean. https://www.youtube.com/watch?v=B3KBuQHHKx0

Anyway, where was I?

Oh yes. Another classic I suggested to Brian Neill, the overall OTMH Producer who was searching for fresh material, was a scene from the spoof western film *Blazing Saddles* where the 'lady' of the saloon sings her rather descriptive song, *I'm Tired*.

I thought the backstage boys had done an absolutely amazing job of building a staircase coming down from a balcony on the stage. The small KNAS orchestra, instead of being located in the orchestra pit as usual, was accommodated stage left, in full view of the audience. That setting was absolutely perfect for a performance by Lili von Shtupp.

I lent the video of *Blazing Saddles* to Brian, who was also an excellent actor and very versatile member of NKAS, to see what he thought. He agreed wholeheartedly that it was perfect material for the show. Then he asked me to do it. The man was mental, of course.

I am not a singer. Oh I can hold a tune, most of the time, but I don't have a good singing voice. But then Lili von Shtupp was no Barbara Streisand either so I really had no excuse. I must have been out of my mind, but I accepted the challenge.

I took down all the words (which I pretty much knew by heart already from watching the movie so many times) before handing the video over to Laura Hunt, the violinist in the orchestra.

The poor woman had to listen to it over and over in order to notate the score for the orchestra, the sheet music being unavailable for that particular song. She did an admirable job.

I also needed to give some thought to my costume.

It should be understood that I used to be pretty skinny in those days, to the point where I was always very self-conscious of my spindly legs which, in my opinion, looked like a couple of matchsticks with doorknobs for kneecaps. There was absolutely no question of me wearing a basque with stockings and suspenders similar to that proudly flaunted by Lili von Shtupp. So I set-to making myself a busty petticoat instead, that I could swish around provocatively.

It was white, trimmed with burgundy ribbon and had a frill around the hem. It was also *very* low cut to emphasise my already more than ample bust. Great care had to be taken with the construction and fitting, as at the end of the song I was tilted horizontally, and the last thing I needed was for my boobs being liberated whilst I was carried off the stage.

[You know it would make this so much easier to describe if you have seen the film, or at least watched that scene. [www.youtube.com/watch?v=Uai7M4RpoLU]

We kept the sketch as true to the film as possible, even to the point of having some cowboys sitting at tables onstage, though instead of four rifle-toting soldiers, we had four chorus-line waiters doing that little march/dance.

The sketch culminated in me falling, like a felled tree, into the arms of those waiters. Being positioned behind me, I shut my eyes every night and hoped they were in the right place to catch me. One night they had threatened not to be, just to see what happened. Thankfully they didn't follow through with it.

How I wish we had a video of that OTMH. I think Ziggy did try to take one, one evening, but sadly the lighting wasn't adequate for our very basic filming equipment.

19
Christmas Capers

At the beginning of December, Ziggy announced that he thought he might have to go off into the bush in the North Western Province of Zambia for a short while.

Apparently, whilst we were on holiday earlier in the year, Ziggy's works had made some huge bolts and nuts for Rhinestone Civils who had a contract to erect microwave link masts across the countryside. The bolts were cast in concrete to hold the masts in place. Alas, when they came to perform the installation, they discovered that the nuts didn't fit the bolts. The only way to find out exactly what was needed was for someone to visit each site and accurately measure up. Because the bolts were different sizes, it meant every single one needed checking. Apparently nobody else in the company had the know-how to do this accurately, so Ziggy decided he'd better do it himself.

He had always fancied a trip into the 'real bush' though I could have thought of better times to do this than December. We reached the week of the 12th and it was decided that he, Peter, and another worker, would go on Wednesday the 14th. This was delayed a day, then another.

I was getting quite upset about the whole thing because they thought they could be away for as long as a week. It meant he wouldn't be returning until two days before Christmas, which was cutting it way too fine for my peace of mind.

You might understand my distress if I tell you that they were travelling in only one Land Rover, and once they had passed through Solwezi, 250 kilometres to the west of Kitwe, they would have no means of communication with the outside world at all. Unfortunately no number of my pleas or tears would persuade him to delay the trip until after Christmas as the Civils were waiting to move back onto their job before the beginning of January.

So it was that on Friday 16th they went off in the company Land Rover. It was loaded to the hilt, carrying:

- five Gerry cans of fuel
- a huge selection of tools to repair the Landy should it break down on the road
- two spare wheels
- hurricane lamps
- a huge tarpaulin (to sleep under)
- three sleeping bags and mattresses
- boxes of food, drinking water etc

- a defunct freezer being used as a cool box

Plus, of course, all the tools and instruments necessary to do the job they were actually going for.

Ziggy called me on Friday night to say they had arrived safely in Solwezi. They were still there on Saturday night, after sorting out the first mast, which was in a different direction to where the majority were located. Early on Sunday he called again to say they were about to set off into the wild green yonder and I should not expect to hear from him again until their return to Solwezi, possibly on Wednesday.

From thereon in, to stop me fretting about what might go wrong, I tried to keep myself as busy as possible. This was not difficult for me.

On the Sunday we had been invited to a *braai* by friends who lived in Kalulushi, half an hour's drive from Kitwe. We drove there at midday but didn't stay long as it clashed with the kids' Christmas party at the Cricket Club. Being a bit late leaving Kalulushi, we drove into the Cricket Club car park, right behind Santa on his train.

I had to quickly get the kids out of the car and tell them to go to where other children were waiting (they wanted to get on board Santa's train) while I tried to park the car in the overflowing car park. I then made a mad dash into the clubhouse (unseen by any kids) to deposit their presents into Santa's sack, which was hidden in the grotto.

Then I went outside to watch all the kids (there must have been over thirty of 'em), who had been shouting for Santa as his train did a tormenting circuit of the cricket field, before pulling up in front of his incredibly excited audience. Their faces were an absolute picture and fair brought a tear to my eye.

Surrounded by adoring, screaming children, Santa *Ho Ho Ho-ed* his way into the clubhouse and disappeared inside his grotto, to be welcomed with a roar when he stepped out with a very large, heavily-laden sack over his shoulder. Then, as he extracted each gift from the sack, he called out the child's name. I had managed to push our kids' presents into the middle, to make the excitement of anticipation last longer.

Once all had received, opened, admired, compared and played with their presents, the games started. Eventually, at 17:30, we returned to our other party in Kalalushi.

We arrived in time to pick at the remains of the *braai* as everyone settled down with cool beers to enjoy the rest of the evening. A couple of people had brought along guitars so a singalong started up and a jolly good time was had by all.

After such an exciting day, the kids fell asleep on armchairs inside the hosts' house and by ten o'clock I was beginning to feel the strain a bit myself. I decided it was time to head home and, after loading the car with our various possessions and the kids, I bade my farewells to the assembly.

Another friend who, in the absence of his wife, was also travelling alone, kindly offered to drive convoy back to Kitwe and make sure that I was 'safely tucked up in bed' before continuing the couple of kilometres down the road to his own house.

When we reached Mwande Crescent, and I had parked in our driveway, I naturally asked him if he would like to come in for a coffee. After I had put the kids to bed we sat in the lounge chatting about nothing in particular when he looked across at me.

"You know, I've always fancied you," he said.

I spluttered into my coffee.

"Really?"

"Oh, yes."

This came as somewhat of a surprise. The gentleman in question whom I think we shall call Arnold, simply because I have never known anyone called Arnold, was pretty handsome and no mean catch for any woman, but he had a stunning wife, who was a lovely lady.

"What say you and I have a bit of fun tonight?" he went on.

Thank goodness I'd finished my coffee, or I might have choked on it.

I figured it must be 'the drink talking', though he was far from drunk. But the reason his wife wasn't there was because she was in the UK, having his baby! I was mortified. How could he even think about having sex with another woman when his wife was probably at that very moment, writhing in agony giving birth to their first-born?

"Ziggy would never know," he continued, with a twinkle in his eye.

"Oh yes he would!" I proclaimed, "because I shall tell him!"

I was perfectly happily married with a more than adequate sex life which did not need enhancing with closet encounters, thank you very much.

Arnold then continued with general chit chat as if nothing untoward had been said.

At the first lull in conversation I swooped on the opportunity to say that I was actually feeling quite tired and it was time he went home. He departed in good spirits. I concluded that it was the beers, together with an enforced abstinence of sexual activity over the previous few weeks, that prompted his advance.

On the Monday I was able to palm the kids off with some friends during the day so that I could get stuck into the mountain of sewing which had to be completed for paying customers before Christmas.

A couple of weeks earlier one of the kids had asked why it was that some people had presents under their Christmas trees before Santa came. We had explained that people did give gifts to each other, as well as getting the special ones from Santa.

Just before they went to bed that night the subject was broached of what they were going to give each other for Christmas. So I let them delve into the very depleted Birthday Present Bag which contained gifts for giving to their friends. Working in secret, Vicki chose a gift for Leon and Leon chose one for Brad. Brad was to choose one for Vicki but the trouble was that there were no more girlie presents left.

After Vicki and Leon had gone to bed I let Brad choose from some nice fabric I had bought in England and from which I would make Vicki a dress for him to give to her. As if I didn't already have enough sewing to do!

Tuesday was their friends, Richard Coote and Jamie Stalker's, birthdays. They were having a joint party to which all our kids were invited. I had already made a sort of karate suit for Richard and for want of imagination decided to make one for Jamie too. When I'd finished that I made a start on some curtains I had promised for a friend.

After lunch I took the kids along to the party then beat a hasty retreat home to finish the curtains and make Vicki's dress while she was out of the way. By five thirty I was absolutely spent and went to fetch the kids from Jenny's house. I didn't take much persuading to stop for a chat and a drink.

It was close to seven by the time we left and I was worried that I might miss a call from Ziggy with an update. I was never so surprised as when I turned into our drive to see Ziggy's Land Rover sitting under the car port. I almost wept with relief.

It transpired that they had finished the job earlier than expected and, apart from a quick petrol stop in Solwezi, had driven flat out from their last remote location back to Kitwe.

Of course, once Ziggy was well relaxed after his trip I told him all about the incident with Arnold. I had thought he would be furious and spoiling for a fight. But the wretch thought it was hilarious.

The next time we were at the Club, Arnold was there chatting with someone at the bar and had his back to us. I watched as Ziggy strode purposefully up to the bar and tapped him on the shoulder. Arnold turned around and although he stood a couple or so inches taller than Ziggy, his face displayed an instant *oh no* look.

Then, taking Arnold's right elbow in his left hand, Ziggy drew his arm towards him – and shook him firmly by the hand!

"I understand you tried to proposition my wife while I was away," he said with a grin. "I would like to congratulate you on your excellent taste in women."

My devoted husband then stayed chatting with him at the bar over a couple of beers!

* * * * *

Dear All,

I thought I might drop you a quick line to let you know what we're planning for Christmas. After the raucous Christmas of '82 at Jane and Robin's house we thought we'd have a quiet lunch by ourselves and then invite some friends to come round later in the afternoon.

The only trouble was I knew that several people were going to our friends, Mairi and Ken Cummins, for lunch but I wasn't sure how many would want to come on to another party after that, so I chatted to Mairi to see what was going on. Mairi was quite keen to have someone else also interested in organising things for Christmas, so we arranged a meeting of a group of us at our house.

I explained my interest in having people round in the evening, but said I'd prefer to be at home for lunch so that I could work to my own timetable. Mairi was a bit concerned that as people transferred from her house to mine some would go astray and that it might also break up the atmosphere to move on.

"Well, seeing as you've got a pool for the kids to play in, rather than us all having to move half way through the day, why don't we have the entire thing at your house?" she asked.

Without really giving it too much thought, I agreed.

A couple of days later when I gave it some serious mulling over I realised what I had let myself in for. I had agreed to have twenty three diners for Christmas lunch as well as a party for god only knows how many more at night. What a twit I am!

Where on earth is everyone going to sit to eat their dinners? It will be very difficult fitting 13 adults and 10 kids around one dining table, not to mention the fight which might ensue over our six chairs!

This is going to take some serious planning.

Fortunately Jane and Robin are going away for Christmas, so I have arranged to borrow garden chairs and table from them as well as their bar stools, drinks fridge and kitchen table. (I declined the kitchen sink.) The good thing is that I can collect their stuff well before Christmas day to save last minute hassles. I have to borrow more stuff from other people but I won't bore you with that.

I'll let you know how I get on.

Anyway, Merry Christmas to you all.

Love,

Me.

* * * * *

Christmas was a blast. We got off to an early start so that the kids had time to play with their presents before it was time to pack the gifts safely away before our guests arrived. Despite the hotchpotch of borrowed tables, our settings were beautifully laid out, complete with imported Christmas crackers and napkins. Food, which had been pre-cooked by the ladies, was kept warm while starters were assembled and roast potatoes completed. We sat down to enjoy our traditional Christmas dinner at 3pm.

This was one of the times when I really appreciated the fact that Benton was a Jehovah's Witness. Not recognising this Christmas celebration, he was available to do all the clearing up as we moved through the courses.

Most folk were on the cusp of the post-Christmas-dinner nap when our other guests began to arrive. Being sub-equatorial, Christmas arrives in the middle of the Zambia summer, so formal attire is hardly the order of the day. Which is fortunate because of what happened to Brian Neil, the first of our guests to arrive.

"Oh that pool looks good enough to swim in," he commented and was promptly pushed in.

Not wishing to be discriminatory, everyone who arrived thereafter also got dumped in the pool, fully clothed.

By the time we'd finished we didn't possess a single dry towel and half the contents of my and Ziggy's wardrobe seemed to have been lent out to people who lived too far away to go home and get changed.

As ten thirty approached, and after a most enjoyable session, we began to shovel people out the gate. We needed to get some sleep as we had planned an early start for the following morning.

20
Siavonga

After the fiasco with our house in the UK, when we went on leave in '82, we sold the property and, what little was left of the sale price, after the mortgage had been paid off, we invested in a Jersey, in the Channel Isles, bank account.

Almost a year down the line my parents were looking at leaving their pub. My dad had developed serious back problems that required major surgery. With only a fifty percent chance of success, he was told he most certainly would not be able to continue with his pub duties.

Bass Brewery owned my parents' pub, my folks being tenants. Alas, they had insufficient funds to purchase a property of their own, now that they had been forced to retire. Ziggy and I decided that, with the money from the sale of our old house and a little help from our bank and my parents, we should buy a property for them to live in.

It transpired that a couple of good friends of my parents were selling their house. We had visited them at some point, so knew a little about the property, and decided to put in an offer, which they accepted. In the November of '83 I flew to the UK to finalise all the legalities required for this deal.

Before I went, I prepared and froze meals for each day I was away, and made arrangements for the kids to go to someone else's house after school. Then, armed with a list of where they went to each day, Ziggy would collect them at five o'clock.

On my return from the UK I was greeted at the airport by Ziggy and the three kids wearing fat grins and holding a banner across their chests reading, *Welcome Home Mummy* in huge colourful letters. Once on the road the grilling started.

"Have you brought anything for me, Mummy?" they all asked in turn.

As Ziggy announced that they had been perfect little angels during my absence I assured them I had bought them all a present which they would get as soon as we reached home.

Ziggy went on to say how well things had gone during my absence and that all the kind souls who had looked after the kids in the afternoons had managed without any glitches.

On speaking to those 'kind souls' over the next few days, all I heard from them was how well Ziggy had managed and how perfectly behaved the kids had been. Ziggy had never once been late collecting them and always made sure all their homework was done. What's more he seemed to have enjoyed it too. It took several days for the kids to get out of the habit of calling me Daddy when they wanted to say or do something.

Talking to Ziggy later, he said he had learnt a lot about his children that he hadn't really noticed before, so my short trip was a 'win' for everyone.

* * * * *

Before I went away there had been talk amongst some of our friends of 'going somewhere' between Christmas and New Year. When I got back I found that a decision had been made to go to a place called Eagles Rest at Siavonga.

Siavonga lies at the foot of Lake Kariba, only fifteen minutes' drive from the dam wall, all very cosy. Except it would take us around five hours to drive from Kitwe to Lusaka, and a further two hours from Lusaka to the Siavonga resort of Eagles Rest. To add insult to injury, the trip had been scheduled to start on Boxing Day. Of course these arrangements were made by *men*.

The participants in this escapade were Jenny and John, with Jenny's two kids and John's parents Eddie and Mac. Then there was Ken and Mairi with Ken's mother, Joyce, and kids Alistair and Clair, and ourselves. The bonus came in the way of Peter. As we drove down in two cars and a Land Cruiser, Peter, delighted at the prospect of a couple of days holiday himself, went on in front with the company Land Rover, stuffed with all our *katundu*.

Ken had been charged with buying all the fresh meat for the duration, Jenny the veggies, eggs, bacon and bread, leaving me to get snacks, canned stuff, biscuits and jams, etc. We also had to take pans, utensils, crockery, glasses and cutlery as the only things provided in the Eagles Rest chalets were beds, a 2-ring electric stove and a fridge. We also took jerry-cans of petrol as we weren't sure if petrol stations along the route would be open on Boxing Day, it being a public holiday.

Peter set off at ten, and despite having ten cases of beer on board, was charged with buying more if he could find any. Ken had run out, as beers had been in short supply before Christmas due to some blunder at Ndola Brewery which reduced output to thirty percent of the norm.

Our departure for Siavonga on Boxing Day was slightly delayed because of a dogfight between me and Coke. I had been in the kitchen putting together food for the journey, which primarily consisted of leftover pork and turkey. While I was dealing with the pork, Coke crept up behind me and snatched the turkey carcass off the worktop. I had not yet got around to stripping the remaining meat from it and we were very reliant on that for our lunch.

As he ran into the garden I raced after him with screams of, "Drop it! Drop it!" grabbing the broom as I went. After a couple of circuits of the pool I managed to corner the thieving hound on the patio. And whilst he did 'drop it', when I went to pick up the carcass, the sod went for me. So I showed him the broom and he scuttled off to the farthest corner of the garden, fortunately minus the turkey.

I picked up the dog-slobbered and dust-covered turkey carcass and headed back to the kitchen, where I rinsed it thoroughly under running water before drying it with paper towel, then stripping off all the meat. I did take the precaution of excluding the bits of meat which had teeth punctures in. Drastic measures, I know, but there was no alternative. Needs must, as the saying goes.

Our little convoy eventually set off at a quarter to twelve and about fifty miles outside Kitwe we passed Peter in the Land Rover. At about one thirty we stopped on the roadside to have a bite to eat. Just before that, we had caught a glimpse of a mass of vehicles parked up on some open ground, which we really didn't give much thought to.

We were about half way through our lunch when they started to drive past. I don't know how many there were, it seemed like about a hundred, but it certainly wasn't less than fifty. And they were all brand new, white, Japanese vehicles which we found out later had been imported via the Tanzanian port of Dar es Salaam and were on their way to Lusaka. Bringing up the rear was a pretty tatty Zambian police car with blue lights flashing. Trundling along behind him came Peter in the Land Rover, with a big smile on his face enjoying, we figured, his police escort.

We cursed ourselves for letting this huge convoy of cars get in front of us. But I tell you what, they weren't hanging around. After clearing up from our lunch and repacking the vehicles, we were 200 kilometres further down the road before we caught up with them.

Even when we had been on one particularly long and straight stretch of road, we could not see the lead car of the convoy. We were very impressed with the organisation and courtesy extended by the drivers, who kept a regulation distance between each car, affording other traffic sufficient time and space to overtake when the road permitted.

As we pulled in for petrol, on the outskirts of Lusaka, the 18 cars we had managed to overtake drove past, with the odd toot and wave, and that was the last we saw of them.

We drove through and out of Lusaka and, after almost an hour, met the mountains and rain of Kafue. The whole scenario reminded me of trips to Wales when I was a kid. Mountains, narrow roads, hairpin bends, grey skies and piddling weather.

It was many miles of diversions over rough muddy dirt tracks and crumbling roads before we saw the first signpost for Siavonga. Twelve miles further on we were greeted by the sign announcing *Eagles Rest Lodge*.

After turning off, we hit the worst stretch of dirt road I had ever encountered, with humps, dips and tilts to left and right. We navigated bends so tight they needed a three-point-turn, and steered around potholes of a size which might swallow up a small cow. We could really have done with being in Lizzy negotiating this lot.

By the time we pulled up outside the Reception chalet it wasn't just the eagles who needed a rest. With money exchanged and keys handed over, we were directed to our three chalets.

Of the three, one had only one room and three beds inside. The remaining two beds were outside on the *stoep* (pronounced 'stoop', Afrikaans for 'verandah'). This chalet was allocated to Jenny and John's party of six.

As we inspected, in the rapidly fading daylight, what would be our home for the next four days, Ziggy made an announcement.

"Well, I don't mind sleeping under the stars. You guys take our chalet which is bigger and we'll take this one."

We shifted beds about, until each chalet had an appropriate number, then unpacked the stuff we had in our cars before settling down with what remained of our cold beers to await Peter's arrival.

Having heard Peter's approach from some way off, we were all out of our seats and standing by the road cheering him in as he rounded the last bend. Then came the big unpack. One of the first things to be located was the big pot of bolognese sauce which had been prepared, as well as my huge pickling pan for cooking the spaghetti.

After a very welcome meal, Peter went off to track down his accommodation and we were all ready to crash out. It had been a long day and we were well in need of sleep. And we were all keen to see what the daylight would present us with.

Naturally the kids were the first to wake and, knowing better than to go exploring without permission, they made sufficient noise to ensure we didn't sleep much longer either.

Lake Kariba was there, though apparently not as full as it used to be when Eagles Rest was first built. There was quite a substantial slope down to the water's edge which was some distance away. We were told that a few years earlier the powers that be had opened the dam's floodgates for a longer period than they should have and, as a result, the water level dropped substantially and hadn't yet had time to fully recover. At least it resulted in a good stretch of beach for the kids to play on.

There was, however, a not-so-good issue with the lake. Bilharzia. This is a parasitic worm which is hosted by certain freshwater snails. When the minuscule worms leave their hosts, they go floaty-swimmy into the big wide water world. Should they come into contact with humans, they burrow into the skin, eventually getting into the blood stream where they procreate. They then get passed out in urine or poo, leaving behind a few eggs to continue the cycle. Those who have been infected over a long time may incur all sorts of nasty problems to the liver, kidneys and bladder. It is known that over 200 million people are affected by bilharzia worldwide. And Lake Kariba is full of the blasted things.

Okay, perhaps that is a slight exaggeration, but they are certainly very rampant in many areas, Siavonga being one of them. We were assured by the Lodge management that the bay in which we were situated was not affected as the snails did not settle in water where there was so much lively boat activity. Either he was right or we were very lucky, because none of our party was affected.

But where was I? Oh yes, the 'beach'.

It wasn't beach sand like you would normally know it, but rather a fine grit with some soil patches. There was also quite a lot of fool's gold (iron pyrites) around. The kids thought this was great and scrounged small cardboard boxes from wherever they could to make treasure chests for taking home.

"It'll make great glitter, Mummy."

In the absence of a power boat for water-based activities, the main pastime was fishing off the rocks. John had brought all his fishing tackle and on the first morning, John's dad, Mac, after first making himself a cup of tea, was making his way to a quiet spot. It had been anticipated that the fishermen would be John, Mac and Ziggy but, after picking up a few tips from Mac, I tried my hand at it. By the end of the first day I was hooked! (Sorry.) Every now and again Ken's son, Alistair, wanted a go and I felt obliged to relinquish my rod, him being *a boy* and all.

The first day had been quite cloudy, so when the same weather appeared the next day we decided to take the opportunity to do a bit of shopping over the border in Zimbabwe where one could get *everything*. Over there we would treat ourselves to things like cheese, chocolate, spices, crackers, soap etc, all the really exciting stuff.

After a leisurely breakfast, we set off and within about 25 minutes cleared the Zambian customs post with relatively little hassle. We then drove over the Kariba Dam wall up to the Zimbabwe customs post. What a palaver we had there. It must have taken us an hour and a half, which was amazing since we were the only visitors being processed. Once the officious little fool condescended to approve one family's papers he would start shooting holes in the papers of another. We thought Zambians were the biggest cretins, when put in uniforms, but the Zimbabweans were far worse.

We eventually left the border post and hastened into Kariba, the nearest town, to go to the bank then do the shopping, only to find that the banks had closed at 12:30 and the shops were closing at 12:45. It was half-day closing there.

Back in the '70s there was a TV programme in the UK where contestants played for a chance to race round a supermarket in one and a half minutes to get as many different things in their trolley as they could, and the one with the highest value got to keep the contents of the trolley. Well, we could have given them a good run for their money. We had five minutes.

Once inside the nearest big supermarket, we each grabbed a trolley and tore round that store pulling anything from the shelves which we hadn't seen for ages. The next hurdle was paying for it, as none of us had foreign exchange and the shop wouldn't accept credit cards. Fortunately John's mum, Eddie, came to the rescue with a load of travellers cheques that we scrounged off her with promises of repayment (at exorbitant interest rates) on our return to Kitwe.

We crammed all the shopping into the car boots, and headed for a hotel. Following a most enjoyable lunch, some of us went off to another hotel, which boasted its own little shop and where we were able to buy clothes. I was very pleased about that as Leon in particular desperately needed some new T-shirts. Because of the formalities involved in cashing more of Eddie's

137

travellers cheques we were very late leaving the hotels and panic began to set in that we wouldn't reach the border posts before they closed the barriers at 6pm.

It was a very close call when we drove up to the Zambian border as they were about to lock the gate. But the promise of a few fresh loaves of bread, plus a few other little treats, paid off and they opened up to let us through. Phew!

What would we have done if they hadn't let us in? Spend the night in our cars atop the dam wall? At least we could have had a picnic with all the goodies we'd bought. The mind boggled, as my dear old dad would say.

When we arrived back at our camp, it took a little while for everyone to calm down. After the drinks cabinet, comprising cardboard box, crates and fridge had been suitably utilised we soon succumbed to the atmosphere of Eagles Rest and resumed the relaxed state we'd enjoyed the night before.

Thursday dawned clear and bright. I spent most of the day intermittently fishing. During one of my absences from the terrace, our dear friends nominated our chalet as the 'party' area for that night. I thought this was somewhat of a misnomer, as the whole trip seemed to be one long party to me.

So after a two-sitting dinner, the first for kids and the second for adults, chairs and tables were carted over to Chalet 10. We started off with a hilarious game of Twister, moving on to a session of Charades, with Ziggy as mediator, while the rest of us leapt about like lunatics. After the kids had gone to bed, we rounded off the night with a few games of cards before retiring around midnight.

On Friday, our last morning, I was awakened by the sun breaking level with my eyes. I leapt out of bed and quietly rummaged around for our camera. I then spent several minutes trying to remember how to manually operate it to capture such a magical scene (previously I had only used it on *auto*).

After several shots at various settings I figured I must have caught something worthwhile and boiled up some water for a cup of tea. Only then did I see the time – it was 5:50. The only time I would normally be out and about at that time of day was if I were going home after a particularly late party!

As I washed my teacup, Mac was up and ready for a fishing session so I decided to get suitably dressed and join him. It was incredibly peaceful with only the sound of birds and the occasional 'plop' as bait was cast into the water. But as the sun rose higher in the clear sky it became increasingly hotter and as I hadn't caught a single fish I conceded defeat, returning to the welcome shade of the cabin area.

By 10:30 we were all packed up and ready to leave for the return slog to Kitwe, which none of us was looking forward to. But the journey was uneventful and we were safely back in Kitwe by 18:30.

An offload of the Land Rover and the dispersal of its contents took place before everyone headed homewards. We were happy in the knowledge that we would all be meeting up the next night to celebrate New Year's Eve at Ken and Mairi's place, as was the tradition.

We sang in our new year at midnight, did some dancing, sang in the UK new year at two o'clock, did some more dancing, and sang in the new year somewhere else, probably Iceland, at three o'clock though I don't think anyone had friends in Iceland, but why not? We eventually pushed off home at about three thirty.

In a rash moment, Ziggy invited anyone who was listening round to our place for New Year's Day and, being a bit tipsy myself, I thought it was an excellent idea. The trouble was that the next morning we had no idea who said they'd be coming. But the first guest arrived before midday and the last left after ten that night.

'Enough already' you would think, but no. As I had forgotten to pack two frozen chickens when we went to Siavonga, we arranged to take them round to Jenny's for a *braai* on the Monday. New Year's Day, having fallen on a Sunday, we got an extra day's public holiday.

Looking back over the whole nine-day experience, it was amazing how 'together' we all were. Nobody fell out or caused upset, quite commendable considering the number and diversity of characters, and three generations to boot.

But it was a long time before anyone suggested a party again.

21
How (Not) to go Camping in Zambia

Dear All,

I say folks, I really am terribly sorry. I just found a letter I wrote to you two weeks ago. I could have sworn I'd posted it, but obviously not.

Anyway it mostly contained questions and having received your latest letter I find you've answered almost all those for me. So here's what else I put in it, which I can now expand on in full, though it might take a while. Sorry.

After thoroughly enjoying the trip to Siavonga, John's parents, Mac and Eddie, wanted to go camping in the bush before the end of their three month visit.

"You know," Mac had said, "real camping. Back to basics."

John suggested Muchia, where he'd been to previously for a fishing competition.

"I won't say the place is basic," John explained, "because there isn't a place as such. It is an area where you can sort of pitch tent and go fishing and stuff."

"But what's there?" I'd asked

"Well ... nothing really, it's just bush. And the river."

I guess you couldn't get more basic than that. This could be interesting.

So we started to prepare for our trip into the *bundu* (another South African term for 'bush'). One of my first concerns were the toilet facilities. We really didn't fancy the idea of squatting behind a tree. The alternative was a hole in the ground but we obviously needed some sort of screen. Jenny suggested using her clothes-horse (a device for hanging clothes to dry indoors) with a sheet draped around it, but I thought that might be a bit flimsy. One good gust of wind from outside (or within!) and it would blow over, exposing the hapless soul trying to go privately about his or her business.

Instead I bought eight metres of green cloth and gave Ziggy dimensions for the poles I needed to support it. A trip to the nearby town of Mufulira, where they seemed to stock a different range of merchandise to Kitwe, was necessary for the purchase of essentials like picnic chairs, paraffin stove and a toilet seat. Then Jenny and I got together to discuss who was to get what in the way of food.

I got all the meat and bread and agreed to make a beef stew for Friday night's supper while Jenny got provisions – tea/coffee makings, eggs, bacon (not counted as meat!) salad, all other incidentals and the cleaning stuff.

We had arranged to borrow a trailer from our friend, Nandy, together with a portable water tank. He also had a tent which he had never used because it didn't have enough poles. He said, other than the doorway, it had a hole in it but was ours to use if we could fix it. So I patched the hole and Ziggy had more poles made up.

The only trouble was we didn't have a tow hitch on Lizzy for the trailer, so one had to be fitted, together with the requisite electrics, the latter being much more of a mission to install.

There were three vehicles being used for this little adventure, John's Land Cruiser, which was allocated to carry his boat, its motor and a fridge. Not a working fridge of course, but the old one which Ziggy had used as a coolbox for his Solwezi trip before Christmas. Mac would be travelling with John. Then Jenny and Eddie along with Richard and Sarah would be in the Range Rover complete with all the bedding. Finally there was us and our kids and just about everything else crammed into Lizzy and the trailer, which we planned to top with mattresses and a tarpaulin.

On departure day, we had to meet up at Jenny's to pack everything appropriately. Just as we began this chore the heavens opened and we had to suspend operations while it lashed down with rain for twenty minutes. We were already running late so this delayed our departure even further. We finally pushed off at about three o'clock.

Being the only one who knew where on earth we were going, John took the lead and we brought up the rear. Lizzy was pretty slow at the best of times but fully loaded and hauling a packed trailer, the most we could reach was 50kph (30mph), or 60kph going downhill. The journey, we were told, should take about three hours, which was cutting it a bit fine to then set up camp before the sun disappeared. The sun, of course, is an essential commodity for providing light. A third of our journey was on proper tar roads but the rest was on dirt roads.

We hit the dirt road after we passed through the town of Luanshya. I say 'dirt road' but that is possibly a bit misleading. This road was well formed and quite wide and was remarkably devoid of the potholes we were used to driving over, round, or into, on our trips through Kitwe. On the downside (literally) it was an odd shape, being quite high in the centre and sloping off to the storm-water ditches on either side. This was to prevent any build-up of water on the road but the trouble was that vehicles travelled at a tilt along it.

One thing that did amaze us was the amount of traffic on this road. Cars, vans, buses, and even trucks, could be seen travelling in the opposite direction. We thought we were heading off to the middle of nowhere and it was difficult to envisage where these were all coming from. We had only been travelling along it for about fifteen minutes when one of the Land Cruiser's front wheels got a puncture.

It took a good five minutes to find the jack and, after John removed the punctured wheel and installed the spare, we discovered that, too, was flat. But it wasn't as flat at the punctured tyre so we decided we could use it, provided it was used as a rear wheel. So then came the extended performance of swapping the front and back wheels around.

By the time this was done, we realised there was no chance of reaching Muchia before nightfall and it would be impossible to set up camp in the dark. At that point I thought we should turn around and go home. John, however, wasn't going to give up that easily.

"There's a boating club just by Luanshya where I'm sure we can set up camp for the night," he said. "Then I can nip into town in the morning and get the puncture fixed. We can be back on the road by 09:00 easily."

So off we set. When we arrived at the boating club we couldn't believe our eyes. It was a proper little resort with a lovely pool, lots of thatched *rondavels* and several play areas for kids; all set on well cut grass. This could definitely not be termed 'camping in the bush'! I said I'd feel like a proper idiot camping there. Ziggy agreed that we should call it off and arrange it for another weekend but was easily dissuaded when John was adamant at sticking it out.

First we had to find someone who could give us permission to use the place. The clubhouse was barred, locked, and bolted, but eventually John managed to track down a bloke who appeared to be the caretaker. He said he thought it would be okay and suggested we went to the power boat section where there were some semi-covered *braai* areas.

We drove around there until we found a nice spot, not too far from an ablution block, then clambered out to discuss the next move. John got stuck into removing all the bedding from the Range Rover so he could access his tarpaulin tent.

We took off the tarp covering our trailer and spread it on the floor (it was the groundsheet for John's 'tarp tent'). John and his dad, Mac, were discussing which way around their tarp should go over the ridgepole when spots of rain the size of bottle-tops began to appear.

We hastily dragged the mattresses from the trailer (no longer protected by our tarp) and crammed them with considerable difficulty (we couldn't open the door very far because of the trailer) into the back of Lizzy. An added problem was that the trailer and Lizzy were thickly caked in red clay dust which we were trying not to smear onto the mattresses.

In the meantime, Jenny and Eddie had managed to chuck their bedding back into the Range Rover while John and Mac had succeeded in hoisting their tarp over its frame only to find that they had put it on the wrong way round. Unfortunately they couldn't remove and reposition it because at that precise moment the heavens well and truly opened.

We herded the kids up to take cover in the *braai* area. This was a structure with three brick walls and a corrugated tin roof. It contained three brick-built *braais* but obviously nobody had given any thought as to where the smoke would go. So the centre roof panel had been removed to allow the smoke to escape, and the remaining panels had rather a lot of holes in them. Eddie and the kids flattened themselves against the walls, rather like colourful embossed wallpaper, in an effort to keep dry.

As John and Mac continued in their endeavours to pin down the misplaced tarp before the increasing wind took it away, Ziggy suggested that I went to Lizzy to fetch our raincoats and gumboots. Yes, we had come prepared! My immediate reaction to decline this invitation was pointless as I was the only one who knew where they were stashed.

I had put them into one of the fitted storage lockers, at the back, so that they would be easy to access, which they would have been were it not for the three mattresses recently stuffed in there. And these weren't just any old mattresses. They were off Jenny's single beds! So I had to take the greatest care not to get my, now, very muddy feet on them.

After removing my shoes I then tried to access the locker which was under the mattresses which were under me. This whole operation took a good five minutes by which time the rain was lashing down like it hadn't rained for ten years. *No way* was I going out in that!

So I fumbled and shoved my way under the mattresses again until I could reach a cool box. Then with a cold beer in my hand, I put on a tape, lay back on the mattresses and listened to music, waiting for the rain to stop. At least five minutes must have passed before the door was yanked open by Ziggy who had squelched his way across the field to collect his waterproofs.

"In case you hadn't noticed, the rain has eased off substantially," he told me.

I can take a hint as well as the next man so I hauled myself up and went outside to take a look. It might have slowed down, but there was plenty of water underfoot. We had chosen a lovely flat piece of ground on which to park, which, of course, meant that there was no run-off for the water. The ground was so waterlogged that it decided it didn't want to absorb any more, and began to create another lake, next to the one with the boats on it.

I rejoined the others to find that John's tarpaulin wasn't as waterproof as he had thought, and the groundsheet under one end of it was already sopping. That was it for me. I quite categorically refused to set up camp there as we wouldn't be able to find an undrenched area on which to pitch our tent.

Apart from that, I could not see the point in setting up a damp camp for one night, to have to pack it away in the morning and drive two hours into the unknown. Then clear bush in order to set up camp again for half a day and one night, and pack it all up again after a few hours 'leisure'. Or was I being a wimp?

"Okay then, let's put it to a vote," said John.

Everyone, bar John, voted that we go home.

By now we realised that it would not be a good idea to put the mattresses back in the trailer because they would get soaked by our saturated groundsheet tarp and, as they wouldn't fit anywhere else, they had to remain in Lizzy. We juggled them around a bit, as much as one can juggle mattresses, so that we could fit our kids back inside without them tumbling down a mattress-mountain every time we hit a bump or a curve in the road.

We set off back to Kitwe and arrived back at Jenny's by 8pm where we immediately set about heating up the stew. With a basket full of hot crusty bread rolls we polished off the lot. It turned out to be one of the best stews I had ever made, so was awarded five stars for the most successful accomplishment of the day.

Of course, the worst was yet to come when we had to face all our friends who had said we were absolutely stupid to go camping in the rainy season, especially with us being complete novices.

My (soon to become ex if she wasn't careful) very good friend Jane Hales was the worst of the lot. When she saw us walk into the Club on Saturday she laughed so much she wet herself and had to excuse herself from work to go home and get changed. Served her right!

For weeks afterwards the witch continued to greet us with, "Hello campers" accompanied by hoots of laughter.

And as if we weren't already really short of storage space in our miniature house, we were now up to our eyeballs with even more stuff to store: tents, toilet seat, poles, pegs and tarps, lamps and a blooming paraffin stove.

Ah yes, the joys of camping.

22
Two Visitors

Dear All,

We had an overseas visitor last week.

A guy called Mike Edwards sent Ziggy a telex to say he planned to visit Kitwe. He was the Africa Regional Something-or-other from the international company which supplies all the bits for the conveyor equipment installed in the mines. Ziggy telexed him back saying he had sorted everything out for his visit and could he please bring with him some cornflour, currants, sultanas and soya sauce!

Mike arrived on a Sunday and Ziggy had arranged for him to stay in the Hotel Edinburgh, our one half-decent hotel in Kitwe, on the Sunday night. Unfortunately they were fully booked for the rest of the week. Ziggy was trying to arrange accommodation at a guest house for the remainder of his stay.

Mike was due to fly into Kitwe's Southdown airport at 9:30 that morning so Ziggy set off at 9:00, taking Brad and Leon with him. I had a phone call from Mike to say he had landed, at Ndola, and that there was no connecting flight to Kitwe, as promised. I told him to sit tight, as we'd sort something out. Five minutes later I had a call from Ziggy.

"You're not going to believe this," he said, "there were no flights booked into Kitwe today so I came to the office. I've been on the phone to Zambia Airways and they said the flight had been cancelled and that Mike is still in Lusaka."

"Well, that's very odd, because I just had a call from Mike saying he's sitting in Ndola because his flight to Kitwe from there was cancelled."

"What the?"

"So you'd better get your ass over to Ndola pretty smartish, kiddo."

Now here's where it gets a bit complicated.

We had arranged to spend the day at a place called Mkoma, which is the location of the boating club we called at on our aborted camping trip. Having seen a bit of the place, between the downpours, we reckoned it would be pretty good for a day out on a Sunday.

Mkoma was about half way between Kitwe and Ndola. You can see what's coming, can't you? Almost an hour later I received a call from Ziggy who had managed to secure the use of a telephone at Ndola airport.

"I've only just tracked Mike down," said Ziggy, "so here's an idea. Instead of coming all the way back into Kitwe, how about we meet you at

Mkoma? You pack all our stuff into the Land Rover and drive up with the other guys."

"That sounds fair enough to me. See you later."

I packed up all our *katundu* into Lizzy and Vicki and I set off to John and Jenny's house. Apart from locking up the house, we found all the parties ready to go when we arrived there.

Hah, were it so simple. We now encounter this particular family's version of departure.

Put the cats out, remember to send the kids (and themselves) to the toilet, put the cats out again, lock all the doors, unlock the door to collect something forgotten, re-lock the door after removing an errant bag from the kitchen, set the alarm, test the alarm to find that something can't be quite shut because the burglar alarm won't activate. Unlock all the doors, track down the offending window which wasn't quite closed, re-lock the doors, unlock a door, put the cats out, re-lock the door, activate the alarm, lock the security gate, and get into the Range Rover.

Our four vehicle convoy eventually left at about one o'clock and it took us three-quarters of an hour to drive there. There we found Ziggy, Mike and the boys, sitting on a sparse bit of grass outside the gates. They had been there, without anything to drink, for over an hour. The security guards of the boating club wouldn't let them in because they didn't have membership cards.

Bloody hell, I thought, *what a way to welcome someone to Zambia!*

Now John and Jenny, as well as Ken and Mairi were members of the Rokana Sailing and Boating Club in Kitwe and since all the boating clubs had a reciprocal arrangement, they could get in. Unfortunately, they weren't allowed to sign in visitors. So it looked like Tom, Karyn, Jamie, Andrew, Ziggy, I and our kids, as well as Mike, were going to be stuck outside. Then John had his brilliant idea.

"I'll explain to the guards that the Patras's have recently joined Rokana but that their cards haven't been issued yet, and Karyn and Tom, you say that you are members of Rokana but you simply forgot to bring your cards!" Mike had miraculously become a member of the Patras family.

Having appeased the guards and signed the Visitors' Book we all piled back into our vehicles and once inside trundled off to look for a suitable parking area. Rather, some of them trundled off. I only got a few metres inside the gates when the Land Rover started to act funny. There seemed to be no power in the accelerator. I glided to a halt then restarted it only to have it fade out again. After several attempts we all came to the conclusion that it wasn't going anywhere.

We eventually found someone with a tow-rope (we actually owned two, both of which were at home!) and got John to tow me with the Range Rover to where the others were parked. It wasn't the best parking area in the place, being some way from the nearest available *rondavel*, but we loaded everyone with gear and carried it to the nearest vacant facility. Then we were able to set ourselves up nicely and the beer flowed freely. That in itself was a miracle as there had been a chronic beer shortage during the past couple of weeks.

Once the Land Rover cooled down John and his dad, Mac, took a look at it and eventually established there was something wrong with the fuel pump, which they couldn't fix.

Shortly after this Ziggy spotted a Rover Zambia Ltd vehicle and went in search of its owner. He managed to track down a bloke who kindly agreed to get our Land Rover towed to the Ndola factory (the one we had bought it from) during the course of Monday, and where we could arrange for its repair.

We had quite a pleasant afternoon, sitting around chatting, whilst the kids, as usual, entertained themselves. But having Mike with us we decided to duck out earlier than usual as the poor soul was starting to look a bit exhausted after his long journey. So we piled into Ziggy's company car and headed home, via the Hotel Edinburgh.

Monday started fairly uneventfully until Ziggy checked again with the hotel and various companies' guesthouses to find there were no vacancies whatsoever anywhere in Kitwe. It became clear that Mike would have to stay with us.

Previously that wouldn't have been a problem, but our Mwande house was beginning to show it's worth, or lack of it. Vicki was relegated to share Leon's bed so that Mike could use her room. And as he was here for a week, half her clothes had to be rehoused into the wardrobe Leon was already sharing with Brad. The word 'crowded' springs to mind.

You would think that after all this, the poor bloke would be very wary about travelling to Zambia again. On the contrary, he said that next time he came out he'd also bring his wife with him.

"She'd love it, especially staying with you crazy bunch!"

We assured him that if he came out again, there was every chance we would have moved into a larger house, where he and his good lady would be able to sleep in a dedicated guest room.

And in case you were wondering, yes, he did bring out the cornflour, currants, sultanas and soya sauce.

* * * * *

You might also be wondering about what happened to Lizzy. Well, I'll tell you.

On the Wednesday morning I got Peter to drive me over to Ndola to collect it. I was expecting to pay anything up to K250, considering they'd had to tow the vehicle from the dam first. When I went through to the accounts office and was shown the worksheet, I was stunned to be told the bill was K344.43. Excluding labour, the new fuel pump which had to be installed had cost K150, which I thought was extortionate, but the avaricious sods had also charged me K160 for towing the vehicle into Ndola.

I let them know exactly what I thought about their bill but decided to pay it and let Ziggy argue with them about it later. He was better at that sort of thing than I was, being a little more diplomatic.

Having received a payment receipt and authorisation slip to remove the vehicle from the premises, the guy said he'd forward a detailed invoice to me later.

"Not a chance," I said. "If I go home and tell my husband I've just parted with K344.43 he'll want to know *exactly* what I've spent it on!"

So I waited for his clerk, who clearly had only one finger, to type it out.

Whilst I waited I wandered back through to the reception area and who should I meet but the General Manager of the place. Recognising me from when I'd visited previously he asked me how I was.

"Stunned," I said.

Naturally he prompted an explanation from me, so I told him. Not only was I disgusted at having to pay K150 for a new part, when I had barely done 6000 kilometres since buying the Land Rover, but to be charged K160 for it to be towed into Ndola was ridiculous.

"It's not *that* far from Luanshya to here," I said.

He thought Rhinestone was paying so I quickly put him straight on that point, saying anything to do with this vehicle was entirely for our account.

"Oh, I hadn't realised that. I'll see what I can do for you," and off he went.

A few minutes later he returned with a revised invoice together with a new receipt and K75 cash refund.

I thanked him graciously and went on my way.

* * * * *

Shortly after Mike returned to the UK we had another pleasant distraction at Mwande Crescent.

We had not been devoid of interesting 'wildlife' back in the Big House, having seen a five inch long stick insect, a baby snake of the harmless variety, and multitudes of geckos and lizards.

One day the kids came racing inside the house to tell me that the dogs had found a big chameleon walking across the lawn, heading towards the rose trellis. I ran and got the camera and by the time I got outside it had already reached the rose bush. I was amazed that the dogs hadn't tried to attack it but the kids said they had simply been following it, peering closely, not quite sure what to make of it. It was larger than anything we'd seen before, its body being about six inches long and its tail about eight inches long which, for most part, it kept tightly curled up. I called for our gardener, Clement, to come and help, having him rustle the far side of the bush while I placed a sturdy stick within the creature's reach. Amazingly the chameleon slowly climbed on the stick, which I took inside where we admired it in comfort. The chameleon, not the stick.

He was an incredibly friendly chap and seemed totally unfazed by our attentions. We were surprised to find that Clement and Benton were absolutely fascinated with him, never having seen one close up before. I would have thought being born and raised in Zambia would have given them many opportunities to see such things. But they told us that most Zambians were really fearful of chameleons, believing that their ability to change colour is some kind of black-magic, so were never encouraged to pursue an interest.

We called the chameleon Clarence.

I held my left hand towards the stick and Clarence carefully inched his way onto my fingers and hand. He sat there quite happily as I slowly walked around the house, occasionally moving his head as if trying to take it all in. It was so weird to have him looking at me with one eye whilst the other was looking at his surroundings. After a while I realised that it was getting pretty close to tea time and I needed to prepare sandwiches for the kids.

As I put my other hand towards him to steer him onto the back of a chair he decided he didn't want that and started to climb over my watch. I moved my right hand closer to him and he began to move a little faster up my forearm. To say I was a little nervous of this is an understatement.

I had never realised the finer points of chameleons before. On the end of his arms/legs, whatever you want to call them, Clarence had hands which were configured like two thumbs and three fingers. On the end of those were long, pointed finger nails. His grip was quite strong and he continued to walk towards my elbow. Before he placed each of his hands down, the tip of his nails would first tickle my skin. It was the strangest sensation which was almost freaking me out. Thankfully he stopped at my bent elbow.

Unfortunately he was in such a position that it inhibited my movements somewhat and making tea was quite a challenge. I had Vicki holding the bread board and Brad gripping the bread as I tried to slice through the crusty loaf like a one-armed man (or woman). Leon was supposed to be suitably positioned in order to catch the slice of bread should if fall off the counter. Instead the little sod was dancing up and down trying not to wet himself as he giggled uncontrollably at our sorry efforts.

In the end I gave up and went back to the lounge where I was eventually able to persuade Clarence to exchange my elbow for a healthy Devil's Ivy plant sitting on the room divider. Tea making then proceeded as tea making should.

Clarence could stay motionless for hours but when the fancy took him he would wander slowly around the plants and shelves of the divider, giving the kids much fun when they returned home from school and played 'hunt the chameleon'.

Because he didn't have much of a natural food source inside the lounge, Rafael, our night guard, would catch crickets, or large green grasshoppers if he could, and put them in an empty jam jar for us to feed to Clarence.

We would lay the jar on its side on a table in front of Clarence where he would watch the contents with interest for some time before, quick as a lightning flash, his tongue would unfurl, reach into the jar and bring out a tasty morsel, recoiling it into his mouth, if it could fit. He would then crunch it up before swallowing.

Vicki, Leon and Clarence

We had wondered why the insects didn't try to jump out of the jar before Clarence got to them and only found out some considerable time later that it was because Rafael had pulled off their back legs to immobilise them, poor things.

Clarence stayed with us for over a week which really surprised us, then one afternoon I caught him swaying across the floor, in the typical cautionary chameleon fashion, towards the open patio doors. He had clearly decided it was time to move on. Perhaps he was bored with his diet, who knows.

Fearful of him being pestered by the dogs, I waited until he'd negotiated the step and then encouraged him to climb onto my hand. (We never picked Clarence up, which would have been an unnatural experience for him, but let him walk onto us if he wanted to.) Calling the kids, I then took him outside the property to a large bush on the other side of our front wall. I held my hand in the centre of the bush until he chose a sturdy branch to move onto.

The kids and I then bade him tearful goodbyes and left him to go his own way. We never saw him again.

23
Here We Go Again!

I had drastically cut my involvement at the Club in the Wardrobe Department, but was still dragged into other activities. One day I recklessly agreed to act in a play, levelled at novices, that was being put on as part of a small festival.

One evening at the beginning of March, I returned home from a rehearsal to find Ziggy in the foulest of moods.

"I've had enough of this bloody place!" he stormed. "Enough is enough! We are leaving here!"

I waited until he'd stopped spitting blood before asking him what on earth had happened in my absence.

"This bloody place is what's happened. I can't find a bloody thing."

A wave of relief swept over me as I realised he was talking about the house and not the country. I was thoroughly enjoying my hectic life in Zambia and was horrified that he might want to leave.

"All I wanted was to make a curry. Nothing fancy. Just a plain old common or garden chicken curry. But could I find the damned curry ingredients? Could I hell. Look at this!"

He strode off down towards the bedrooms and I followed. I was not too enamoured by the sight that greeted me. Half a dozen cardboard boxes were scattered around the passageway, blocking the route to the bedrooms, and the contents of two of the boxes were strewn all over the floor.

"How am I supposed to find cumin, coriander, turmeric and cardamom amongst the rest of all this?" he raged, waving his hand at the mess.

"Well, you won't find them there," I said, "because I packed them all into a shoe box and put it at the back of the grocery cupboard."

I went into the kitchen, removed tinned beans, pickles, jams, cans of corned beef, vinegar, peanut butter, tinned apricots and my precious golden syrup from the bottom of the cupboard before hauling out the shoe box.

"Look, I've written *Ziggy's Curry-Making Stuff* on it" I said proudly.

"And what exactly is the point of *that*, if I can't see the blasted box for the rest of this rubbish? Why didn't you put it at the front?"

"Ziggy," I looked him in the eye. "You can't put *everything* at the front of the cupboard. Something has to be at the back."

"Well, not my blasted curry makings," he snapped.

"Okay then, next time you can't find the pickled onions, don't come complaining to me. They'll probably be hiding behind the curry box! So if it's not chicken curry, what's to eat tonight?"

"Marmite on toast. If you can find the bloody Marmite!"

We had eggs.

After he'd had an hour to calm down we got to talking about this rather unsatisfactory arrangement.

"We can't live like this," he said, "I have made up my mind, we're going to have to find a bigger house."

"Rhinestone are going to *love* us," I muttered.

"That's as may be, but when I've worked hard all day and want to come home and be creative in the kitchen, I don't expect to have to play hunt the ingredients every time."

(Creative curry-making, that was new.)

"Yesterday," he went on, "it took me ten minutes to find a clean pair of underpants in what purports to be our wardrobe. We had more space than that in the broom cupboard at the Big House! And it's not just the storage. I'm none too happy that we only have one bathroom either."

Secretly I was delighted that he had got himself into this state of agitation. The lack of storage space had been driving me nuts ever since we moved in and we'd accumulated even more stuff since then. But had *I* been the one to complain …

And so it was that we were on the lookout once more for a new home, but this time Ziggy was actively involved. We found a huge place on Pamo Avenue, quite close to the town. The configuration of the rooms was such that we were sure it had once been two houses which had been knocked into one.

But the main prerequisites were there. It had four bedrooms, two bathrooms, a big kitchen, a swimming pool and oodles and oodles of storage space. The lounge was huge and there was a separate dining room. It also had two rooms which we couldn't really classify, but were sure we'd be able to fill them with something. Yes, one would definitely become my 'sewing room' I decided.

Ziggy had to do a lot of begging and pleading with both Rhinestone and the owners of the house to secure the place at a rent acceptable to both parties. The only down side was the servants quarters. They were much smaller than what Benton and his family currently enjoyed. I didn't feel at all easy about asking him to 'down-size' when we were 'up-sizing'. After much discussion it was agreed that we could increase the size by adding an extra room to the *khaha*.

Ziggy borrowed the services of a bricklayer from our friend, Nandy, and hired two casual labourers to help him. They were all about as much use as a chocolate fireguard. I think the extent of the bricky's knowledge went as far as mixing cement and smearing it onto bricks. The more complicated aspects, like laying foundations, placing *compatible* bricks together and marking a straight and level line to work to, seemed a little beyond his expertise. It appeared that it was down to *me* to make sure he was told exactly what was required and precisely how to do it.

Fortunately Ziggy and I had done a lot of improvements to the house we bought when we first got married, so I wasn't completely blind to the intricacies of such matters.

I had been hoping to move into the new place before Vicki and Leon's birthdays at the end of March, but this additional work now put paid to that. Supervising building work (every couple of hours or they slackened off), as well as organising food for about twenty kids (plus a few adults) for a party on the forthcoming Friday, was hectic. I also had to make four birthday cakes, one each for school (they were in separate classes) and two for home. I didn't believe they should have to share a cake at their party just because their birthdays were on the same day. Packing up an entire household in the middle of all that, ready to move out on the Saturday after the party, was pushing it a tad further than I was prepared to go.

Then I hatched a cunning plan. We would hold a Packing Party. I would invite all our friends on the Saturday and *they* would do the packing for us! Then all we had to do was to move it all on the Sunday when Ziggy was off work. Except that it turned out virtually all our friends, including ourselves (I had forgotten), had been invited to a *braai* at Jane and Paul's place on the Saturday afternoon.

But I wasn't going to let a little thing like that faze me. We'd do it on the Sunday instead. It meant all our possessions would actually be moved on the Monday morning.

As the packing party was a truly original idea (as far as anyone knew) I found plenty of suckers keen to take part. People were trembling in anticipation of being invited to such a prestigious event, or so I'd like to believe. So out went the invitations.

The party must have been about twenty strong. People started to arrive at about 14:00 and we began in the socially acceptable norm of waiting around the bar, with a few beers of course, until everyone had arrived, so that we could suss out who was going to do what.

There were bodies all over the place, cardboard boxes galore and one of the brightest of the bunch had brought along tons of shredded paper for packing the delicate stuff. (Bubble wrap was still in its infancy and certainly hadn't yet found its way to Zambia).

Kids were banished outside, though not before they'd managed to grab armfuls of the shredded paper to shower each other with around the garden.

Then we got stuck in.

There was Lynn Quarmby doing ornaments; Ken Cummins was on books whilst his wife Miari was packing crockery and glasses; Jenny and John were in the kitchen boxing up food items. Somehow the two Janes, Hales and Kelly, also managed to fit in there to sort out the kitchen equipment.

George Carr and Pat Banda dismantled and folded up all the curtains; Robin Hales was responsible for crating the stereo and video equipment; Maureen Carr sorted out the bathrooms whilst Maureen Bentham wrapped up the pictures.

Crispin Quarmby and Tom Stalker packed up all our clothes leaving poor John Bentham to search out and box up all the kids' toys. Karin Stalker's important duty was keeping the kids occupied and out of the way. Ziggy was in charge of the bar, though we weren't sure whether he was re-stocking, packing, or drinking it dry.

INVITATION

YOU ARE CORDIALLY (DESPARATELY) INVITED TO

A "PACKING PARTY" AT OUR MWANDE HOUSE ON

SUNDAY, MARCH 25TH AT APPROX. 2:30PM

DRINKS WILL BE PROVIDED BY THE FOREMAN AT

REGULAR INTERVALS, AND FOOD BY THE FOREWOMAN

ON COMPLETION OF WORK.

PLEASE BRING YOUR OWN GLASS, PLATE AND KNIFE & FORK

AS HOPEFULLY ALL OURS WILL BE PACKED.

ACCEPTANCE OF THIS INVITATION IS CONDITIONAL

UPON GUESTS SUPPLYING ONE SIZEABLE CARDBOARD

BOX AND ONE OLD NEWSPAPER, PER PERSON.

~~NUTTERS~~ KIND PEOPLE WSHING TO PARTICIPATE ARE

ASKED TO PLEASE RSVP TO AP ON 214370 ASAP.

DETAILED JOB DESCRIPTIONS WILL BE ISSUED ON ARRIVAL.

As General Foreman I wandered from room to room generally sorting out queries and keeping everyone supplied with packing tape, scissors and marker pens. I also had one very important task, that of announcing the beer breaks by switching on the burglar alarm siren every hour. The neighbours must have wondered what the devil was going on!

We were all finished by six o'clock. I had made a huge pot of beef stew the day before, to be accompanied by potatoes and crusty bread. The only trouble was it must have been one of my best ones because it was gobbled up so fast that Jane Hales, Ziggy and I didn't get any. But thanks to neither the deep freezer nor the microwave oven having been packed, we were able to tuck into some pork rissoles and mushy peas after everyone else had left.

It was agreed by all that having a Packing Party had been a brilliant idea to the extent that some were considering moving house so they could have one too. By the time we hit the sack that night I was absolutely exhausted.

Ziggy went off first thing on Monday morning to organise transport at the Rhinestone offices. Whilst he was gone I loaded up the Land Rover with the boxes of delicate stuff and, with Clement helping me, offloaded them all into the Pamo Avenue house. Leaving Clement there, acting as day-guard, I returned home to find a flat-bed Rhinestone truck parked in the drive, which was shortly joined by Ziggy and Peter, both in company *bakkies*.

It took two truckloads, two more Land Rover batches and three *bakkie* loads to move all our possessions from one house to the other. Because Ziggy was anxious to get vehicles and people back to work, everything was just dumped anywhere inside the house. The only things which were put in the appropriate rooms were the beds, lounge and dining room suites.

Peter returned with a *bakkie* in the evening to help Benton move his stuff.

All the boxes of stuff had been quite basically labelled with their content or location but, as I hadn't actually packed much of it myself, I didn't know exactly what was in each box.

It took a good couple of weeks to finally place everything in our big new house and thereafter it was a dream.

Of course, we all know about dreams. Eventually we have to wake up to reality.

24
Carry on Camping

Apart from fascinating things like moving house we were determined to continue with our new hobby, camping. Yes, once again we were off to spend some quality time with tents, basic cooking facilities, ad hoc meals, uncomfortable beds, communal toilets, and ants.

Our first attempt had clearly fallen under the heading of 'Failed'. But I have never been one to baulk at challenges, so I was quite happy to give it another shot.

Whenever someone new arrived, so did an inevitable question.

"I see you have a Land Rover. Do you do a lot of bush driving?"

Receipt of a negative response to that elicits another inevitable question.

"Ah, you go camping then?"

Really more of a statement than a question. Receipt of another negative response usually elicited a couple of nods accompanied by an expression that indicated he or she realised they were now talking to an idiot. It didn't seem important that this was the only vehicle we could buy which had wheels and an engine that (sometimes) worked.

I must also admit that the motivation for this determination to try our hand at camping again was sparked by the fact that we had just bought a tent. A guy who was leaving Zambia, came into the Club one day and was desperate to get his hands on a bit of cash. He was willing to sell his continental tent for a low price. He wanted K400 for it, which in real terms of the day (black market money) worked out at £66 (US$95), a very good price. He assured me that it was a good one and in excellent working order. Ziggy and I scraped together and handed over the cash and he dragged the tent over. I then took it home and tried to put it up, tried being the operative word.

Returning home from the club after a few beers, Ziggy refused to help. I struggled with all the poles (I calculated there must be about 500 of them) but was unable to connect them to resemble any normal sort of tent shape. I postponed my efforts until the next day.

On the Sunday morning, with a much clearer head, I managed to sort it out with no trouble. I almost managed to pull the canvas onto the frame but eventually had to enlist help with this.

Surprisingly, it turned out to be a beauty. It had an enclosed bedroom area which was split into two sections that could sleep Ziggy, me and the three kids quite comfortably. We could even manage three adults in each section if necessary without being too up-close and personal. I was very relieved to find that we hadn't bought a dud.

Having got the gear, all we needed now was a bit of enthusiasm from our friends, and for the rains to stop.

In the interests of practicality we thought Easter might be a good time to go, but we decided that our first long weekend attempt should perhaps be at a recognised location. So we chose Mulungushi Dam.

It was a flipping long drive, four and a half hours, but we figured it would make us feel like we were really *going camping*. Of course, it wasn't *real* camping. There would be no *bundu*-bashing or anything so rough. The fact is it was home to the very civilised Mulungushi Boating Club.

The logic behind this choice of venue was that they had a clubhouse with a bar that was open all weekend, which meant we wouldn't have the hassle of sourcing, storing and trying to keep chilled sufficient beers to keep us going for a long weekend. And it had a nice swimming pool, which the kids would appreciate as they weren't allowed to swim in any of the local dams in case of crocodiles and bilharzia.

As we drove there on the Thursday afternoon, the sun was shining in a clear blue sky and a little breeze rustled the elephant grass along the roadside. We arrived at the dam at 3pm to find we were the first campers there, so had the pick of the site.

We climbed out of the vehicles and, stretching our aching limbs, were nearly bowled over. The gentle breeze more closely resembled a force eight gale. I'm sure I don't really need to say any more, but I will.

The first stage of erecting the tent turned out to be very easy, chiefly because prior to dismantling the tent in our garden I had marked all the poles and connecting angles with numbers and letters so that I'd know how to put it together the next time. I had even made a little sketch indicating the location of these letters/numbers. Smart eh?

The trouble was I must have blundered somewhere along the line because I had some numbers twice, and a couple of poles which didn't appear to fit anywhere. I didn't recall there being any spare parts the first time.

And of course the Lord of the Manor was of no use at all, having had nothing to do with it previously. After fumbling about for twenty minutes I eventually got it looking something like a tent frame, only to find that we'd left a crucial angle unit at home.

It had broken when I'd dissembled the tent and, after getting it repaired, it wasn't put in the right place, namely in the tent bag! So the master of ingenuity had to step in and stuff bits of wood and bent tent-pegs into the poles and strap them together with odd bits of string before we could call the basic framework 'finished'.

Then the fun started. We succeeded in draping the canvas over the half-height frame but every time we tried to lift it from half to full height some of the blooming legs fell out. Each of the legs came in three sections, joined by internal springs. Or they were meant to be. Obviously some of these springs had sprung and disappeared.

We eventually succeeded by having a person at each of the seven legs and simultaneously lifted on the count of three; whereupon everyone disappeared under the flowing canvas like a sequined assistant under a magician's cloak. Escaping the shroud, Ziggy and John hastily began to peg the canvas to the ground whilst Jenny, Eddie and I, still underneath, secured it to the frame with the strategically placed canvas ties. Ziggy and I then managed to fasten the inner bedroom unit in place and *voila!* One continental tent for the use of.

In the meantime our friends had managed to erect their frame quite easily but were having trouble with the canvas. So we tried to help. Just as we got their canvas over the frame, and John was about to hammer in the first peg, a terrific gust of wind hit it and nearly took us all skywards.

I had visions of a tent-shaped kite taking off, with people dangling from each corner like streamers. Then, as the wind abated, the lot would be dumped in the dam as crocodile fodder.

As luck would have it we just managed to stay on *terra firma*, albeit a couple of yards further away from where we'd started, only to be informed by the peg hammerer that the tent was facing the wrong way. The openings of the other tents faced into the laager we had formed, whilst this tent's door overlooked the ablution block. Not the most salubrious outlook. With additional helpers, we hoisted the complete unit off the ground and quickly turned it one hundred and eighty degrees until it faced the right way.

Last to go up was John's tarpaulin which was to act as a giant shade-cloth for us all. This entailed Ziggy climbing trees to secure two corners of the tarp whilst the other two corners were supported by poles. The only difficulty was that the tarp was slightly wider than the horizontal pole set between them, so couldn't be ideally secured.

Finally we got the rest of the communal gear set up in the gaps between the tents in a very well-organised-looking fashion.

Actually, we were fortunate that no other campers had yet arrived to witness the pathetic state we had got into before we finally achieved that impressive appearance. Having said that, it still wasn't too late for me to make a complete ass of myself.

By Friday lunchtime, because of the wind, the tarp had come a little bit adrift. We tried re-lashing it but it didn't make much difference so I eventually moved Lizzy round so that the front of the tarp could be secured to the roof and rear door. This worked well as it also gave us a bit more flat work space if we left the rear door open. By late afternoon Ken was getting a bit alarmed by the way the wind was buffeting his tent. As it got worse towards late evening he pleaded for Lizzy to be moved back where she was originally, as she had been acting as a wind-break for his tent.

Yes, you've guessed it. Whilst I remembered to unhitch the tarp from the back door, I forgot it was also secured to the roof. I drove off with the tarpaulin stretching out behind me and everyone screaming at the tops of their voices for me to *stop!*

Luckily I did so before any serious damage was caused and quickly reversed so that the tarp could be safely unhitched. A borrowed pole and another length of rope eventually fixed the overhead tarpaulin and the Cummins family could sleep in their tent safe in the knowledge that they wouldn't be blown into the dam during the course of the night.

All in all, our camping expedition was deemed a complete success, with adults having a wonderfully relaxing time whilst the kids made loads of new friends. Packing up on the Monday afternoon was far less strenuous than setting up, though not nearly so much fun!

* * * * *

You may be wondering why I am always harping on about crocodiles.

I do have a fascination with this ancient reptile, although my observations had so far been confined to the comfy seat of a safari vehicle, as I am under no illusions regarding the danger these creatures present.

One weekend during our first year in Zambia, we went with friends, Steve and Jan, to a place several kilometres outside Kitwe. It was a small nature/leisure/fishing lodge set on the banks of the Kafue River. The park contained several chalets which, we were told, could be hired per night for a very reasonable amount. And whilst surprisingly intact, they appeared not to have been occupied by anyone for a long time.

At strategic points there were brick-built *braai* boxes for visitors' use with plenty of mature trees for shade. We found ourselves a lovely spot to settle down near the river, though not too close as we didn't want the kids to go near to the water. To be fair they were becoming very good at listening to instructions regarding safety, so when we explained that we had been told there could be crocodiles in this river they kept well away from the water's edge. Anyway, there were plenty of open spaces where the kids could play with ball or frisbee, as well as a basic play area with swings and seesaws.

The nearest any of them got to the river was when Brad briefly ventured half way down the slipway from which fishermen could launch their boats into the river, though we didn't see anyone with boats that day. In fact, we didn't see many people at all, but we had a very enjoyable time.

Three weeks later we heard about a most horrific occurrence. A family, like ours, had gone there for the afternoon and their son had been playing on the very same slipway Brad had walked onto. A crocodile came out of the water, up the slipway, then grabbed and dragged the child away into the river.

The poor child never stood a chance. When crocodiles snatch their prey, usually from the water's edge, they drag it under the water to drown it and if not devoured immediately will stash it in underwater lairs for later consumption.

Despite frantic and thorough searches of the river and its banks by fishermen and game experts, the child's body was never found. It was the most horrendous thing we had ever heard. I cannot begin to imagine how the parents coped with such a tragedy.

Needless to say, we never returned.

25
Health Wave & Pork Pies

Finally things were coming together. We were nicely settled in our new home, everything had its place and we knew where to find it. With 'smooth' being the word of the moment any level of sagacity will tell you that something was bound to come along to screw it up.

On the Monday after Easter, Ziggy announced that he was feeling 'a bit off'. He complained of flu-like symptoms, aches, hot and cold sweats, etc. He put if off for as long as he could but eventually consulted the Company Clinic about it on the Friday. He arrived home midmorning and announced that he had been diagnosed with hepatitis. We had obviously heard of it but didn't have a clue what to do about it. Ziggy had, of course, been told odd bits by the doctor but, being a typical male, I couldn't get much sense out of him. I phoned my friend Jane because she knew just about everything.

"Ah, that'll be him off the booze for six months then," she said.

I also sought out a more professional response to my queries and phoned the Clinic. I was told that there was nothing much that one could do to assist the hepatitis victim. He just had to 'rest it out'. I was told that he should not eat a lot of protein-rich food whilst the infection was strong, which meant no meat, fish, cheese, butter, milk or eggs.

Great. That meant that all he could eat was potatoes, other vegetables, fruit and bread. And Zambia happened to be experiencing a flour shortage at the time, so bread was in short supply. Alcohol was a definite no-no. I asked if there were any long-term after-effects of hepatitis and was advised there were none, provided he stick to the rules. So there began the longest 'holiday' Ziggy had ever had. The doctor immediately gave him a three month 'sicknote' for his employers.

At around the same time, Vicki had been having trouble with tropical boils. All the kids had had their fair share of these over the past couple of years, being very common in the tropics. But Vicki's weren't responding so quickly to the regular treatment, an applied paste of magnesium sulphate. I decided to take her to the doctor. She had also been suffering with hot and cold spells and sleepiness but, as she didn't have a high temperature, I had put it down to another one of those phases kids go through.

I was just beginning to explain to the doctor why we were there when he received a phone call. Of course, I couldn't help but listen in. The call was from someone at the Theatre who wanted to know if they should go ahead and serve food at the upcoming Awards Ball which had been prepared by someone who was thought to have hepatitis. During the conversation the doctor went on to describe the symptoms of hepatitis and as he did so I was looking at Vicki. One of the clues was a yellowing of the skin, which naturally was quite difficult to discern on a suntanned body. Another giveaway was the colour of the whites of the eye. The doctor put down the receiver and turned to me.

"Forget about the boils for a moment," I said, "do you think she has hepatitis?"

"Good Lord, yes!" he said, after the quickest glance at her.

The whites of Vicki's eyes were the colour of custard.

Anyone with half a brain would think I should instantly have realised Vicki was suffering from the same thing as her dad, but one rarely associated child and adult illnesses. A couple of weeks later Brad also had it. We were told someone could be infectious for up to four weeks before the symptoms appeared. The good news though, was that children didn't suffer as severely as adults.

Apparently the hepatitis A virus is transmitted through ingestion of contaminated food and water, and possibly saliva. In a slim effort to avoid Leon and I catching it we were advised to keep the eating implements and cups/glasses of Brad, Vicki and Ziggy separate from ours.

So I got three full sets of cutlery and wound a piece of black insulating tape around the handles, as well as making a black cross of tape on the bottom of their cups, mugs and glasses. For several weeks these were always washed separately to the other dishes. Leon and I were spared the wrath of the virus.

Within a six week period there was hardly a single expat family in Kitwe who didn't have at least one family member affected by it. But no-one ever figured out where it began although a lot of our friends had been to a mutual friend's party, from where we suspected the big spread had originated.

No sooner was Vicki back to normal than I had a phone call from a friend to say her daughter, who Vicki had recently been playing with, had got mumps. Two days later Vicki went down with it on one side of her face. Whilst feeling generally okay she said her face was a bit sore. No sooner had that improved when the other side of her face became swollen, though not so sore this time, she said.

Ziggy continued his recovery but after a few weeks was getting bored with lazing around in the sun drinking vast quantities of water. He started doing odd things around the house and walking into town which, since our recent move, was now only a few hundred metres from where we lived. It didn't take long for him to realise this was not a good idea, that his system really wasn't ready for it.

One thing noted was that it could not have been a better time for him to get hepatitis because if he had been fit and well his beer drinking would have been considerably curtailed anyway. There was a gross shortage of beer on the Copperbelt, and not enough in Lusaka for their brewery to want to send any in our direction. Sad days indeed because with that situation the beer drinkers were turning to drinking spirits, causing shortages for the normal spirits drinkers. I have learnt over the years that such situations do not sit well with expatriate communities.

I seemed to be spending quite a lot of time in the kitchen. This was mostly in an attempt to provide varied meals containing ingredients which were within Ziggy's very limited diet at the beginning of his convalescence period.

One day, with the kids accompanying me to the town bakery, I bought them some doughnuts. I was absolutely appalled at the high price and low quality. I mentioned it to Jane and she said she could make doughnuts, and promptly produced a batch for the kids to try. They went down like hot cakes. (Sorry!)

I offered to pay her to make some more but she declined the privilege though did kindly give me the recipe. Of course, me being me, I had to go and try making the ones with the jam in the middle, didn't I?

The recipe said to have the oil hot to the point where it was just starting to smoke, and then to put the doughnuts in and cook them for about three minutes.

After about twenty seconds my first doughnut resembled a perfectly round piece of charcoal, so I took that out and turned the heat down a bit. A few minutes later I tried my second doughnut and this time it took about 30 seconds for it to produce a perfectly round piece of charcoal.

I thought to myself, *there's something wrong here, I'm sure they should come out a lovely golden colour.*

I took the pan off the heat and waited for the oil to cool down for ten whole minutes. My third doughnut stayed in for a minute and a half before turning a dark brown colour, at which point I removed it.

I thought I'd better test it before I went any further and found that it was still a bit doughy in the centre so waited a bit longer for the oil to cool and then maintained it on a low heat. I think I finally cracked the temperature problem, the only problem was that with the outside of the doughnut cooking more slowly, it didn't seal in the jam, and as the doughnut slowly swelled to the correct size, the jam equally slowly oozed out. That was when I understood why Jane had made *ring* doughnuts.

After that I sussed the system and made perfect batches of ring doughnuts until everyone was sick to death of eating them.

Another thing my dearest friend Jane taught me was how to make pork pies. We usually made them at her house and I became quite an expert at it. My first attempt at making this culinary delight was quite an experience. In case you should ever want to treat yourself to one of these amazing comestibles I shall give you the instructions.

Dear Reader, do not be fooled into thinking that what follows is a regular recipe. Things were never that straight-forward in Zambia.

MRS HALE'S PORK PIE

1 lb lean pork
½ lb pork sausage-meat

½ tsp pepper
½ tsp salt
2 pinches mixed herbs
1 tbsp water
12 oz flour
5 oz lard
½ tsp salt
¼ pint water
1 egg
2 x 1lb loose-bottomed pie tins, (4½" diameter)

If you don't have any 1lb pork pie tins, improvise. All I had was a loose-bottomed cake tin (7-inch diameter) so I decided to make one big pie instead.

Hurdle Number 1: the Zambian butchers at that time did not sell sausages. If you wanted sausages you had to make your own sausage-meat. I did, and usually had sausages in the freezer. Of course, Murphy's Law kicked in as I found I had run out of sausages, so I first had to get more pork with which to make the sausage-meat. Did you notice how easily I said that? Do not be fooled.

First you have to remove all the fat from the pork, and I mean *all* the fat, because if you don't it clogs up your mincer. Yes, I am talking about an old-fashioned metal mincer. The one you clamp to a table or counter top, then stuff the meat into the top funnel and crank the handle until your arm nearly drops off.

Cut the pork into small pieces. Mince it. This can take several hours because you usually find that you didn't manage to cut off all the fat after all, and as it goes through the mincer the sinewy bits stretch over the holes making it impossible for the meat to pass through.

You then put all the minced pork into your blender and whizz it up until it gets really mushy. During the course of this procedure you need to occasionally switch off and pry the unwhizzed bits out of the corner, getting your hands covered in sausage-meat, where it gets stuck into your rings which you had forgotten to remove before the start of the operation. Remove rings, wash. Continue to whizz

By the time you have got your sausage-meat, to which you have added breadcrumbs and your imported sausage spice (for heavens sake don't forget that) you have gone right off the idea of making pork pies. However, perseverance being the word of the day, one must continue.

Next take your half pound of cubed pork and half pound of sausage-meat and place it in a bowl together with the salt, pepper, herbs and water (not the ¼ pint, that's for the pastry). Mix all this together with your hands, which you have only just washed sausage-meat off.

Before doing this, you will have (haven't you?) remembered to place another large mixing bowl in the oven to warm up into which you have put the flour and salt. If not, wash your hands again and carry out the above.

Back to the meat.

Complete mixing your meat whilst shouting for someone else to answer the ringing telephone. Scrape meat mush off your hands, wash roughly and go to answer the phone yourself which will, by the time you have reached it, have stopped ringing.

Wait by the phone for two to three minutes because you know it will ring again. Answer the phone and engage in a ten minute conversation, most of which is spent explaining why you were so long answering the call.

Once back in the kitchen remove the bowl of flour, which by now is very hot, from the oven.

Place your five ounces of lard and quarter pint of water into a saucepan and bring to the boil. Pour the liquid into the flour and mix together with a round-bladed knife. Soon comes the point when you can no longer mix with the knife and you have to use your hands.

You are roughly up to your elbows in it when it hits you that the combination of hot fat, water and hot flour isn't the best thing to put your hands into. Hold hands under cold running water smartish.

Logic triumphs and you decide to tip the contents of the bowl onto the counter where you will have more room to move and it will cool the mixture down to a more workable temperature. This was a good idea until you realise that you forgot the bowl was also very hot. Hands under cold tap again.

With the help of a towel or oven mitts, upend the bowl of pastry mix onto the counter and knead contents together quickly. You will find the 'quickly' bit comes quite naturally. You should eventually end up with a nice smooth ball of warm dough. Take approx. one third of this and put it back in the mixing bowl to keep warm.

You now have to get this two-thirds lump of pastry to line the base and sides of your tin. This is not as easy as you think because you can't use a rolling pin. Reason – dough sticks to the counter or pin and you're not allowed to add any more flour to make the procedure easier.

Instead you squash it into a pancake with your hands and place it in the tin. It is, of course, too small to reach up the sides of the tin as well. Using your knuckles try to ease the pastry across the bottom of the tin and up the sides. Although you can't imagine why, you may find that you have a rather thick wedge where the sides meet the base of the tin. Try to press this out with a little more knuckle manipulation.

Once the pastry is plastered up the sides of the tin, repair the holes which have now appeared in the bottom. Pinching the pastry together usually works.

You are now ready to put the meat into the lined tin.

By this time your pork/sausage-meat mix will have developed a healthy crust from having been exposed to the combined heat of the kitchen (remember your oven is still blasting away at 205°C/410°f/Gas 6) and the ambient air temperature in Zambia of 35°C (95°f). Remix meat to absorb crusty bits. Place the meat evenly into the lined tin. It should reach up to the top edge of the pastry wall. Scrape and wash hands.

You are now ready to fit your lid.

You have already run your fingers/knuckles around the top edge of the pastry wall to make it nice and flat to support the lid. Okay, if you haven't, then do that first. I'll wait...

Now take the remaining lump of dough, which is no longer warm but is rather solid. Try to work this back into a malleable state. Make a lid-sized pastry pancake and lift it over the tin. This could take a while. Don't worry if bits fall off the edge, this is normal now.

Finish off the lid by placing the bits which dropped off, back on, patchwork style. Just as the patchwork is coming together nicely you will remember that you should have brushed the top edge of the pastry wall with beaten egg to make it stick. Don't worry about it because there is *no way* you are going to work that lid a second time if you remove it.

Very carefully, so as not to collapse the wall, pinch round the edge of the pastry to give it that pretty fluted effect that pies always have. Brush the top with beaten egg and think about decoration. Get the bits of pastry which are left (and there are rather a lot of those) and make some quaint little leaves and place them on top, also brushing with beaten egg.

Now you are ready to bake for half an hour at 205°C/410°f/Gas 6, then a further 1½ hours at 180°C/350°f/Gas 4.

Whilst this is going on you may now relax with a couple or so glasses of wine/gin and tonic/¼ bottle of scotch/bourbon, or whatever.

I hope you remembered to set your timer.

At the appropriate time remove your beautifully golden baked pork pie/s from the oven and leave in the kitchen to cool for a couple of hours. Relax a little longer.

Now for the final touch. Take a quarter pint of pork stock, which you just happen to have handy, and warm it up. Pour this into a jug into which you have placed a teaspoon of gelatin and watch as it congeals in the bottom as you remember that you should *always* sprinkle the gelatin onto the hot liquid, never the other way round. Throw that away and warm up another quarter pint of pork stock, if you have any left, which is unlikely, in which case use chicken stock. This time remember to sprinkle the gelatin on the top and stir it around for what seems like hours until all the little crystals have dissolved.

Next you have to pour this through the hole in the top of the pastry which you forgot to make when you put the lid on. Take a sharp pointy knife and try to break a small hole in the top of the rock hard pie crust without caving in the whole lid. If you are DIY minded I suppose you could use a power drill.

Finally pour the liquid into the hole. If you miss and it goes all over the top of the lid don't worry too much, but with a little perseverance and a lot of ingenuity you should manage to get at least half of it inside the pie. Then put the pie in the fridge (probably overnight) to wait for the jelly to set.

Hey Presto, next day you have a delicious Pork Pie.

Of course, I don't make one very often.

26
Here, There and Everywhere

If you thought we'd already done enough moving around since arriving in Zambia, don't bother to unfasten your seat belt.

Whilst Ziggy was off work with his hepatitis recovery, he had plenty of time on his hands to sit and think.

At the start of his second two year contract with Rhinestone he was handed an ailing company to work on. Before the first year was out he had turned an inadequate manufacturing parasitic section of the parent company into a highly profitable Manufacturing Division.

What was he going to do when he returned to work, a fully fit man? There was certainly no challenge left in his current position, and from what he knew of what the parent company was working on at the time, he couldn't see anything in the offing, well, nothing which would keep him revved up, anyway.

So he began checking out the national newspaper for options.

One Sunday when we were enjoying a few drinks and a *braai* with friends, the phone rang. It must have been about 8:00pm and it was some chap called Siame from Lusaka about one of the jobs Ziggy had recently applied for.

Apparently this guy was coming up to Kitwe on Tuesday and wanted to meet Ziggy for an interview. They fixed the time for 11:30 that day. The only trouble was that Ziggy had written off for a couple of positions and didn't know which one it was for. The only one he could think of was for a General Manager of a company in Kitwe, but thought that unlikely.

The next day Ziggy had a call from a guy called Roger who worked for the Mine, and who had asked Ziggy earlier in the month if he would be interested in applying for a job that was coming up there. Whilst this job was for the Zambian Government owned ZCCM, who didn't offer so many perks as the private sector, they were offering very good money, payable in pounds sterling. Roger was phoning to say that Ziggy had been allocated an appointment for the Tuesday afternoon. Being on sick leave he had no trouble keeping these appointments.

It seemed Ziggy was in hot demand, and he was dead chuffed about it!

It transpired that Siame was the Chairman (CEO) of a company called Siame Associates (Zambia) Ltd. That was the holding company for a group of companies ranging from a large construction company and several engineering companies (refrigeration, asbestos, mining and railway supplies, etc). There were also trading companies and a pharmaceutical firm – the list went on and on. The fact that Siame was also the owner of SA(Z)L seemed incidental.

Apparently he was currently trying to fill three positions, one being General Manager (GM) of a constructions company, another was Assistant GM of an engineering/manufacturing company and the third was GM of the Management Services Division (MSD) for the Group.

At the interview he told Ziggy all about each company and the positions involved. He went on to say that he felt Ziggy was too young to be offered the position of General Manager of the construction company (it was a big one) but asked him which of the remaining two positions he fancied.

Ziggy told him that he didn't really like the idea of being an Assistant General Manager, as he preferred to be in charge rather than having to act on someone else's decisions, but that he did rather fancy the position of General Manager of the Management Services Division. So Siame gave him the job. There and then! On the spot!

As I'm sure you can imagine I was speechless (well, almost) when he told me all about it. Even Ziggy couldn't take it in.

The Management Services Division dealt with all matters relating to special projects, marketing, everything necessary for imports and exports, and goodness knows what else, in an advisory capacity.

Ziggy had taken with him a breakdown of what benefits and perks he was currently receiving from Rhinestone and gave it to Mr Siame to see if he could match or better it. Does an eagle fly?

He said it was Ziggy's choice as to whether he be based in Kitwe or Lusaka. Whilst the majority of the group's companies were based in Kitwe Ziggy immediately thought that he would be better positioned in Lusaka where he would have more immediate access to all the government administrative departments he would be dealing with. A Lusaka base would also be more convenient for the International Airport when it came to receiving the anticipated plethora of overseas visitors.

Mr Siame told him he would need to find himself a house.

"Buy one if necessary, appropriate to the position, namely five bedrooms, pool, servants quarters, etc. and furnish it as you please."

Oh boy, was I ever going to have a field day.

Later in the week I was talking to some acquaintances who were visiting Kitwe. They had recently moved to Lusaka themselves.

"You'll have quite a job finding a house in Lusaka," said Farida.

"Unless you've got someone on your side with a fair bit of 'clout'," Mo agreed. "Who's he working for?"

"The Management Services Division for a group of companies," I said. "The bloke who owns the whole bang-shoot is called Siame."

"*The* Siame? Well, you'll definitely have no trouble then," said Mo, mightily impressed.

So just six months since we had moved house, we were going to be doing it again, only now we would be changing company and moving city too. As much as they enjoyed the last packing party, our friends were quite relieved to hear that this time Ziggy's new employer was paying for professionals to do the entire removal.

You would think, then, that everything was hunky-dory and a smooth transition was the order of the day. In the Patras household? You have to be kidding!

Before all this came to the forefront we had been trying to finalise arrangements for, not only our end of contract leave to be taken, but also for my mum and dad to visit Zambia for a few weeks. My dad had recovered well from the surgery on his back, or as well as he ever would. Now that they were enjoying full retirement, my folks had plenty of time to fit in a trip to Africa.

We had been planning to take three weeks' leave to the UK in late July so the idea was for them to come over on the same flight we would be returning on. The arrangements were already being complicated by Zambia Airways changing their fleet to accommodate fewer but larger intercontinental aircraft, and for some reason this also affected the ticketing classifications and seat allocations. Now it was to be further complicated by a house move. But it didn't stop there.

All shades of the brown stuff were flying around Rhinestone. One guy (Ziggy's immediate boss) was leaving (under a bit of a cloud) and a few of the engineers were not renewing their contracts.

The result of all this was that Ziggy's application for leave to go to the UK was denied by the top boss. Ziggy didn't rock too many boats about that because he had managed to secure a few days' leave for our planned game-viewing trip.

Oh, I didn't mention the game park yet, did I? As my mum had enjoyed her first visit to one back in 1981, and my dad hadn't yet been on one, it was a given that a game-viewing trip would be taking place during their stay with us. Our friends Lynn and Crispin were joining us on this trip and, as we had all been to South Luangwa National Park several times, we decided to give Kafue National Park a try this time.

Whilst I didn't want to go without him, Ziggy insisted the kids and I still went to the UK on holiday in July, returning to Kitwe with my parents in tow.

But I'm getting a little ahead of myself here.

One of the things that I needed to organise before our move was a replacement for our trusty house servant Benton. I had broken the news to him that we were moving and that, when we left, he would receive good redundancy money and excellent references. I told him that if he wanted me to, I would also put the word out that he was going to be looking for a new job.

I wrote out an advert for Ziggy to place in the Times of Zambia giving job specifications and reference requirements for Benton's replacement in Lusaka. I had decided that this time I really wanted to get a house-servant who could cook basic meals too and gave an indication of the salary on offer for the right person.

When I went out later that morning I left the advert details on a coffee table, waiting to hand to Ziggy later. After a few hours I returned home and was approached by Benton.

"Madam," he said, looking rather nervous, "I must talk to you."

I thought maybe he'd broken something, or wanted some time off.

"What is it Benton?"

"I would like that job in Lusaka."

"I beg your pardon?"

"I would like the job for you in Lusaka for more money."

"But the reason it is more money, Benton, is that I want someone who can cook," I explained to him. "And remember I did promise that when we leave here, because you have worked for us for three years, you will receive a bonus for losing your job. And I shall give you excellent references."

"The madam can teach me to cook. I can learn very fast. I want to still work for the madam."

I was flabbergasted.

"But what about your family? They are here, and all your friends and your church," I asked him. (Benton was a very active Jehovah's Witness.)

"My family will be happy to come with me. And there is a church for me in Lusaka."

"Let me talk with my husband about it Benton. I'll let you know."

Wow! I hadn't expected that!

Ziggy was equally surprised when I told him.

"Well, if you're happy to teach him to cook, and at least you know he'd do it the way you want, I really can't see any reason why he shouldn't come with us. He has proved to be very reliable. But let me first speak to the boss."

Ziggy duly spoke to Mr Siame who was quite happy about it, saying the company would pay for Benton and his family and possessions to travel down by train to Lusaka when we were ready.

So now our move to Lusaka consisted of Ziggy, me and three kids, our three dogs, my mum and dad and a family of seven (Benton had racked up 5 kids by this time, from the original two he had when he first started working for us).

Our journey home from England was one of the most uneventful I had ever undertaken, most probably due to the calming influence and help of my mum and dad. In Kitwe, my mum, Nancy, did a lot of catching up with the friends she'd made when she had visited back in 1981, as well as being introduced, along with my dad, Mev, to a host of other friends we had made in the subsequent three years. The sad thing was we would be leaving all these friends behind in Kitwe in a couple of weeks.

While I'd been away, Ziggy had been able to get one of Mr Siame's people to search around the housing market. The guy found a couple of places but recommended one he thought would be preferable. It was a regular four bedroomed house but with the addition of a good sized guest suite. It was set in almost an acre of walled grounds and was located in a nice area. Whilst Ziggy hadn't seen it he agreed to take it on the basis that it couldn't be all that bad, as the previous person living there was the Governor of the Bank of Zambia. I won't insult your intelligence by quoting all the quips and jokes our friends made about that, because I'm sure you can imagine!

Disappointingly the property came furnished, so I was denied the shopping spree I had been looking forward to, other than to buy a couple of extra beds, which didn't really require much imagination.

* * * * *

Our trip to Kafue National Park was, by comparison to South Luangwa, quite a disappointment. The accommodation was actually outside the park's boundaries and was no more than adequate. Each time we wanted to go game viewing we had to enter by the main gate, paying a nominal fee. The gate was only opened at 06:00 and promptly closed at six in the evening.

When we had been to South Luangwa, Mfuwe Lodge had been inside the park, where you could find some animals in the lodge grounds. In fact, the first time we arrived there, there was an elephant wandering through the car park!

Kafue was the largest of Zambia's National Parks and, whilst it was home to all the regular species of wildlife, they were more spread out. The game rangers knew the regular haunts of the different species. But we went game viewing in our own vehicles, rather than with organised trips and as a result saw little of great interest. Later I heard that the better areas were to the north of the Park, not where we had been. However that did not stop us from still having a very memorable experience.

During the course of conversation with some people at the lodge, we heard about a couple of young bull elephants who inhabited the area. Apparently they were not too enamoured by the moving metal machines which travelled through their domain and had been known to charge at these unwelcome intruders.

"It is best to give them a wide berth," we were told.

But these weren't the only elephants in the area, so we asked how we would be able to tell which ones they were talking about.

"You can't mistake these two," said Johan. "One of them has only one-and-a-half tusks."

Our questioning looks prompted the answer.

"They had a bit of a fight one day and one won, the other lost ... half a tusk. Ha! Ha! Ha!"

We figured that if one could break the other's tusk in half, and they were the best of buddies, we wouldn't like to get on the wrong side of them.

On the afternoon of our last day, only half the party wanted to go out game viewing. As I had been the one doing the driving in the Land Rover, Crispin suggested that this time I be a passenger.

The professional rangers' vehicles were generally open Land Rovers with tiers of seats in the rear. We would use Crispin's vehicle in similar style by putting our canvas fold-out picnic chairs in the rear of his *bakkie*. With Cris and Lynne in the cab and Mev, Brad and myself seated in our picnic chairs, we set off.

If the park officials at the gate thought there might be a problem with our travelling arrangement they certainly didn't bother to tell us about it as we handed over our couple of *kwacha*.

It didn't take us long to find that the chair arrangement didn't work quite as well as we had hoped. Every time Crispin veered even slightly to the left or right so did the chairs. We clearly had not given much thought to Newton's Laws of Motion when we designed our temporary game viewing arrangements. The state of the road didn't help either.

Our amateur game warden (Crispin) drove as fast as road conditions would allow, which was open to some interpretation. Whilst at the main point of entry the road was fairly wide and clear, it was corrugated with ridges, similar to the rippled pattern left on a beach by cross currents of water, but bigger. Driving over these while sitting in a vehicle's seats you wouldn't notice them too much. But we were sitting in lightweight metal-framed chairs on the metal floor of the *bakkie*. As the vehicle juddered over these small ridges we were being shaken silly in the back. I felt like a gold nugget in a giant riddle.

In the absence of any anchoring equipment, like a few good lengths of rope, our chairs also jumped and tossed us around as Crispin came into contact with the all-too-frequent potholes. We clung to the sides of the *bakkie* as if our lives depended on it, which they probably did.

We eventually reached the point where the road split in two, almost like a very lengthy railway siding. It rejoined the other road a few kilometres further along. We decided to take the right-hand road, which lay nearest to the lake.

Two days earlier, when we were out on a morning ride on this road in the Land Rover, we had caught sight of Bill and Ben, the two grumpy juvenile elephants, but they had been some distance away and we didn't hang around to get a closer look. We guessed they had been drinking at the lake which lay behind them.

On this particular afternoon, despite Crispin having slowed down considerably, we didn't see anything along that stretch. Once we branched away from the main track we travelled on for half an hour, seeing an assortment of African buck, baboons, warthogs and zebra. We even saw a couple of giraffe in the distance.

After half an hour, we reached the point where we needed to turn around and head back to the main gate. This time when we came to the fork in the road we chose the one to the right, furthest from the lake.

The return journey is invariably shorter than the outward one as we no longer were scanning the long grass, bushes and trees for signs of four-legged or brightly plumed creatures. It subsequently came as quite a surprise when about 100 metres away, and a little to our right, there suddenly appeared, from behind some large bushes, the ominous figures of Bill and Ben.

If this had been a 'B' grade movie there would have been a sharp squealing of tyres as we screeched to a halt. In real life that doesn't happen on a dirt road. What does happen is a dry-earth skid and a cloud of dust, accompanied by a lot of unrepeatable expletives from the driver and passengers. Had they not already seen us, this would definitely have alerted Bill and Ben to our presence.

We looked at them and they looked at us. Very carefully Crispin selected the reverse gear and very, very slowly began to back away. At the road, the elephants crossed the *donga* in one stride, mounting the slope onto the road in another. With two tusks to the fore, they stood with their ears wide and their trunks waving in the air before one emitted a trumpet blast that any brass band would have been proud of.

Maintaining the flapping ears and raised trunk posture, they began to walk towards us. Crispin drove a little faster. They continued to walk, and Crispin drove faster still. Their walk got faster. You would be absolutely amazed at how much ground an elephant can cover at a walk.

Every vehicle has its speed limit, and we were quite surprised how fast a *bakkie* travelling backwards could actually go. But at the rate those two big boys were accelerating it was never going to be fast enough. Crispin decided he needed to make use of his four forward gears.

We were all competent drivers (apart from Brad), so doing a three point turn would not normally faze any of us. But doing it on a dirt road, which sloped steeply down on either side like a tiled roof, with two bull elephants charging down on you, can put you under a bit of pressure.

We had been travelling more or less, given the fact that we were going backwards, in the centre of the road so when Crispin came to a stop he didn't have the full road to initiate the three-point-turn. As the three points turned into five, these two giants were closing in fast. By the time Crispin took off in a forwards direction they couldn't have been more than forty metres away and gaining.

I don't think you can begin to imagine the fear generated by being stuck in the back of an open, low level, flimsy vehicle with two enormous elephants, each reaching at least ten feet in height and weighing in at about five tons, bearing down upon you.

Crispin put his foot to the floor and we shot off in a cloud of dust, initially unable to see if the elephants were right behind us or not. As the dust cleared we could see they had come to a stop and we in the back were able to draw breath again. But that didn't stop the shakes we had all developed. And believe me, they had nothing to do with the state of the road!

As Bill and Ben disappeared, you would have thought this was the time to get out and remove our tarnished underwear. But the fun wasn't over yet. We still had to get out of the park before the gate was locked for the night, and we were travelling in the wrong direction.

We continued to drive until we reached the point where the two roads merged into one, then did a hairpin turn into the road which ran closer to the lake.

There was one slight problem with taking that road. At some point on their way to the water, which logic told us was where they were ultimately headed, Bill and Ben had to cross this road too. We had no idea how long it would take them to reach the second road. If they had traversed the intervening bushland at a normal walking pace then they should have crossed the road well before we reached that point. On the other hand, if they had stopped for a tasty bit of vegetation here and there, or a scratch up against a hefty tree along the way, then they might still have to make that crossing.

The trouble was we hadn't been paying that much attention to the distance we'd travelled along in the other section of the 'siding' when we met them the first time, and certainly weren't paying any attention to the odometer when we left it. So we had no idea how far along this road they might appear.

We were beginning to see signs of dusk, with lengthening shadows darkening the undergrowth. It was pretty dense hereabouts, with low trees and high bushes, and there wasn't much open space between the thicket and the road. What I'm saying is that we mightn't get much warning should Bill and Ben suddenly appear on the road.

To use a few succinct words, we were terrified. But luck was with us and we did not encounter the pair again, and we made the Park closure with ten whole minutes to spare. But we were still very shaky when we hit camp.

A fair few whiskies were downed that night, I can tell you!

27
And Next... ?

On our return to Kitwe life became very hectic as Ziggy finished off all his work related issues and we finalised our plans for the move to Lusaka.

Spending those few days with Lynne and Crispin brought home the fact that I was leaving behind in Kitwe a lot of very good friends and I would miss them tremendously. I had thought the same when we left England four years ago but, in retrospect, apart from family, there were only a couple of dear people who I was very close to. The friendships I had made in Zambia were also 'different'.

When we first arrived, the expatriate community in Kitwe was quite large, so there did tend to be different groups of people who stuck together. But barring a few exceptions (there's always one isn't there) there was no rivalry or upset between those groups.

It hadn't taken long, once I got settled into this unusual way of life, to realise that there was something very special about the people who chose to be expats so far away from home. They certainly had to be quite tough, and also very flexible. The ability to take on a challenge, whatever it might be, was essential. Fragile people, or those who constantly harped on about wishing they were back home wouldn't last long. We lived for today, and a little bit of tomorrow, but didn't dwell on the past. And we were there for each other when help was needed. Barring a few exceptions, the expat community was very close.

Even before Ziggy started looking around for a new job, we did notice that the Kitwe expat numbers were beginning to dwindle. As the engineers and other specialists in their field came to the end of their contracts, they were being replaced by Zambian personnel who had been trained to take over. People were told that their positions were being 'Zambianised', the official term used.

One of our friends who would not be leaving was Nandy Kovac. We became involved with him at the Theatre Club a few months after we'd first arrived in Zambia.

Nandy was Hungarian, and had lived in Zambia for many years. His English was good but still heavily accented. To increase the difficulty in understanding his accent, he'd had a laryngectomy just before we met him and at that time was still learning to speak again. So the gulped words, mingled with his accent and the frustration at being so incapacitated, initially made him very difficult to understand. Fortunately, over those few years we spent in his company, he became more accomplished and could communicate more than adequately.

Nandy was a character of note who, despite his health situation, smoked cigarillos on a permanent basis and loved his brandy. He had a well-tended, jet-black moustache which he trained with a sliver of beeswax until each side culminated in a cheeky twirl. Where other males may affect personal mannerisms, like stroking a beard or brushing aside a stray forelock, Nandy's trademark was to raise his eyebrows and with thumb and forefinger, give a twist to his twirl.

He was quite the entrepreneur too. He had a catering business which supplied two small café type outlets, as well as assorted club or corporate functions; he made the best biltong in Zambia; had a mobile casino; and he made concrete building blocks. He also loved horse racing and was a consummate gambler. Luckily he was one of the few gamblers I knew with that vice who didn't wreck his fortunes with the habit.

Nandy was the most amazing man, and he offered to organise a special treat of a pig-on-the-spit for our leaving party, the weekend before we departed. Our little 'do' was to be held on the Saturday evening. We had all been out the night before so I wasn't too pleased when Nandy was honking his horn outside our gate at 5:30 in the morning.

"I need to get this pig spitting!" he shouted from the roadside.

The metal spit unit itself was an amazing though simplistic structure. It was designed by Nandy, and I believe Ziggy provided some assistance in its construction. It had two rows of racks to contain charcoal, set low on the base of a frame and a channel about six inches wide lay between them. Above that a pig (or goat) skewered on a long square pole, would be hoisted onto the stand. There were different levels for the stout skewer to rest upon, depending how close you wanted it to be to the coals. An electric motor turned the spit. Then above the rotating meat would be another narrower channel. The entire unit was half-enclosed with a back board and hood. I was informed that this masterpiece was made entirely out of some of the Mine's 'left over' stainless steel.

A large enamel jug of a magically seasoned baste was poured into the top channel, where it would drip through holes onto the meat. As the meat turned and the juices dripped off, they were caught in the base channel, which was slightly tilted so that the juices drained down to be collected in a second jug at the lower end. This was then poured back into the top channel and so the process continued.

But Nandy didn't do things by halves. The skewered pig was stuffed with two chickens, which in turn were stuffed with lemons and herbs.

As the hours of cooking slowly passed during the day, the aromas emanating from this racked feast were amazing. I felt quite sorry for our neighbours, none of whom we knew, who must have been driven crazy by the evidence of this impending feast wafting over their garden walls.

That day was like being on a car journey with the kids. Instead of hearing, *are we there yet*, calls of, *is it ready yet* could be heard. As well as an array of salads there were also loads of large potatoes, protectively wrapped in tin foil and left to bake alongside the coals of the spit.

It was about 6:00pm by the time we ate and the deliciously juicy pork was the best meat I have ever tasted. Of course, it was accompanied by loads and loads of crispy crackling.

All the friends we had met over four amazing years in Kitwe were there to party with us. We had an awesome night, with singing and dancing, and everyone certainly made it a send off to remember.

Another event to be covered that week was very special.

Our recent trip to the UK meant we missed the final week of the kids' school year in Lechwe. During that time the school's Prize Giving ceremony had taken place. Unbeknownst to him at the time, Leon had been awarded a prize for Excellent Achievement in All Subjects in his Class (1 Hippo). Our friend Jenny Coote had kindly offered to arrange a special Prize Giving just for him at the school. The fact that school was officially closed mattered not, given that Jenny was the headmistress.

Headmistress Jenny Coote presenting Leon with his prize

It was a lovely presentation, with some of our friends and kids attending, as well as Leon's teacher. Leon was thrilled to bits and we were very proud of him. We all thought this was a super gesture by Jenny and a wonderful way for our children to leave their first school in Zambia.

Two days later the removals company's truck was at our house to pack us up. What a pleasure it was to leave everything to the experts. That same day I had to take the dogs to the local boarding kennels. The kennels were run by the local SPCA and Nina, the lady in charge, had agreed to organise the transporting of our dogs down to Lusaka.

Dog crates, especially big-dog crates, were in short supply, so the dogs were to be freighted down one at a time. Special arrangements were made to ensure each dog was fed and watered during the journey, which took about 24 hours. We arranged for Bass to be sent first. Once he had been collected, the crate would be sent back on the next train to be used for Coke, this procedure would then be repeated for Sally, before the crate was finally returned to the SPCA for future use by other dog owners.

By the end of the day, all that was left to pack into our car and Lizzy were the clothes we had held back to keep us going for a couple of days, our bedding, a few glasses, mugs and tea-making equipment and toiletries. And ourselves. The removals van had been parked in our driveway overnight for security.

Departure day arrived. At six-thirty we were about ready to leave. Rafael, our trusty night guard, had waited beyond his normal departure time of 6:00pm to say goodbye. He would still have work with Rhinestone's security section, guarding another household in Kitwe, after our departure. As we said quite an emotional farewell to Rafael, we presented him with a bonus of *kwacha* equal to over two months' wages which we felt he deserved after keeping us safe at night for the two and a half years he'd been with us.

The truck driver started his engine and we climbed into our vehicles. My mum and Leon travelled with Ziggy in his company car whilst my dad, Brad and Vicki joined me in Lizzy.

We followed the truck through the very quiet streets of Kitwe until we reached the open road to Ndola. As Kitwe slowly faded in my rear view mirror, I brushed away a couple of tears before overtaking our life's possessions and heading towards the rising sun.

Then, turning right at Luanshya, we began the long journey south to Lusaka, and whatever life held for us there.

If you enjoyed this book, I would be so grateful if you left a review.
Thank you!

To be informed about Ann Patras's new releases, please email
Annpatras.author@gmail.com
Contact welcome!

About the author

Ann Patras was born and raised in Burton upon Trent in the English Midlands. Ann's life was always crammed with people, originally through her family's busy corner shop, then at her parents' pub and later through her own varied careers.

After raising three kids, countless dogs and living in Africa for over thirty years, Ann and husband Ziggy, over 40 years married, now live in Andalucia, Spain and have absolutely no intention of ever moving again.

Contacts and Links

Email
Annpatras.author@gmail.com

Blog - The Crazy World of Ann Patras
http://annpatrasauthor.com

Ann Patras on Facebook
https://www.facebook.com/ann.patrasauthor?ref=ts&fref=ts

The 'Africa' Series on Facebook
https://www.facebook.com/AnnPatrasAfricaSeries?fref=ts

Ant Press Books

If you enjoyed this book, you may also enjoy these Ant Press memoirs:

Into Africa with 3 Kids, 13 Crates and a Husband by Ann Patras

Chickens, Mules and Two Old Fools by Victoria Twead (Wall Street Journal Top 10 bestseller)

Two Old Fools ~ Olé! by Victoria Twead

Two Old Fools on a Camel by Victoria Twead (thrice New York Times bestseller)

Two Old Fools in Spain Again by Victoria Twead

One Young Fool in Dorset (The Prequel) by VictoriaTwead

Midwife - A Calling by Peggy Vincent

Fat Dogs and French Estates ~ Part I by Beth Haslam

Fat Dogs and French Estates ~ Part II by Beth Haslam

Simon Ships Out: How One Brave, Stray Cat Became a Worldwide Hero by Jacky Donovan

Smoky: How a Tiny Yorkshire Terrier Became a World War II American Army Hero, Therapy Dog and Hollywood Star by Jacky Donovan

Instant Whips and Dream Toppings: A True-Life Dom Rom Com by Jacky Donovan

Heartprints of Africa: A Family's Story of Faith, Love, Adventure, and Turmoil by Cinda Adams Brooks

How not to be a Soldier: My Antics in the British Army by Lorna McCann

Moment of Surrender: My Journey Through Prescription Drug Addiction to Hope and Renewal by Pj Laube

Secondhand Scotch by Cathy Curran

Serving is a Pilgrimage by John Basham

Chat with the author and other memoir authors and readers at **We Love Memoirs**:

https://www.facebook.com/groups/welovememoirs/

12214927R00106

Printed in Great Britain
by Amazon